Row 1

-213 -243 -141 -229 -254 -128 -198 -237 -94 -223 -220 -274 -296 -92 -129 -303 -137 -3 -329 -340 -281 -8 -212

Row 2

-330 -H. Reynolds -314 -A. McRae -134

Row 3

-138 -273 -183 -219 -139 -228 -279 -221 -205 -267 J. Brown -242 -257 -227 -161 -290 -253 -83 -300 -163 -241 -11 -294 -140

-E. E. Elliot crew -320 -261 -239 E. E. S. Freeman crew -165 -319 -316 -315 -308 -201 -323 -E. W. King -304 -260 -17 -143 -149 -250 -37 -32 -313

Drawing courtesy of Mr. Frank W. Robinson, Digby, Nova Scotia

The *Titanic* victims graves in St. John's Methodist United Cemetery

Graphics by Annie Lokuta

Roster of Valor

The Titanic Halifax Legacy

Roster of Valor

The
Titanic Halifax Legacy

by Arnold and Betty Watson

NAUTICAL   PUBLISHERS   BOOKSELLERS   IMPORTERS

7 C'S PRESS, INC.

P.O. BOX 57
RIVERSIDE, CT. 06878, USA

TABLE OF CONTENTS

ARNOLD WATSON
1905-1984

This book has very special meaning. It is, firstly, an informative guide to the gallant men and women who comprised the crew of the White Star liner *Titanic*. It is also a chronicle of the important role in the disaster's aftermath played by Halifax, Nova Scotia. But especially, this volume will stand as a lasting and final tribute to the memory of a gentleman from Pottstown, Pennsylvania whose consummate interest in the ship and her people—and whose never-failing generosity—made this work possible.

Arnold Watson was born on May 12, 1905 in Middleport, Pennsylvania. A graduate of Pottstown High School, he went on to receive a certificate in accounting from the Wharton School of the University of Pennsylvania, Reading branch. From the mid-1940's until his retirement in 1964, he served as treasurer and sales manager for the U.S. Axle Corporation in Pottstown.

In his spare time, Arnie (as he preferred to be called) became actively involved with a large number of national and local civic, fraternal and church groups. And with his wife, Betty, he loved to travel.

Arnie loved history, too. He was a member of the Society of the Sons of the Revolution, the Pottstown Historical Society, the National Railway Historical Society, the Berks County Historical Society, the Valley Forge Historical Society, and the Daniel Boone National Foundation.

It was almost inevitable, then, that Arnie's interests in history and travel combined with a lifelong fascination with *Titanic*. In 1972, Arnie and Betty joined the Titanic Historical Society, and soon thereafter made a research trip to the city of Halifax, seeking *Titanic* information.

Two years later, Arnie personally published his "*Titanic* Crew List" as a gift to the THS's membership. The 44-page booklet, done after extensive researching and cross-checking of many sources, featured the first alphabetical listing of the ship's crew, their home addresses and ratings, and a special section devoted to the Watsons' Halifax visit.

It was to be just one of the Watsons' many generous acts to benefit the Titanic Historical Society. In 1976, Arnie and Betty made a sizable grant to the Society to ensure its continuing, active role in preserving and disseminating *Titanic* history.

For his outstanding contributions to the Society, Arnold Watson was made an honor member of the organization in 1977.

In 1978, Arnie was asked to serve as chairman of the Society's advisory board. In 1980, he was appointed to fill the unexpired term of vice president Charles Haas, who had assumed the post of president upon the passing of William Harris Tantum IV. Arnie was re-elected to the position of vice president in 1982.

That year—the 70th anniversary of the *Titanic's* foundering—proved to be a milestone year for the Titanic Historical Society, in large measure due to the Watsons' continuing faith in the organization. On April 15, the Society's archives, after years of private storage, at last went on public display at the Philadelphia Maritime Museum. The Watsons' 1976 grant had made the archives' establishment possible.

Another special grant allowed two of the Society's officers to go to Halifax for ten days of intensive research. The resulting Spring, 1983 issue of the Society's journal contained significant revelations about the lost liner and its Halifax connections.

In 1983, in honor of the Society's twentieth anniversary of founding, Arnie and Betty, with another bequest, set into motion the production of this volume, a revised and expanded *Titanic* crew list, to be presented to every Society member.

Tragically, Arnie was not spared to see the completion of *Roster of Valor: The Titanic-Halifax Legacy*. On April 21, 1984, just one week after the anniversary of the *Titanic's* fateful collision, Arnold Watson passed away at Pottstown Medical Center at the age of 78.

While Arnie steadfastly refused public acknowledgment of his and Betty's many outstanding deeds of generosity and support, the Titanic Historical Society's officers believe it only fitting and proper that this volume be dedicated to the memory of Arnold Watson, gentleman, friend and benefactor, whose support of the Society in word and deed will be so deeply missed.

Charles Haas
President
Titanic Historical Society, Inc.

FOREWORD

by Walter Lord

When Arnold and Elizabeth Watson compiled their alphabetical list of the *Titanic's* crew in 1974, it seemed the final word on the subject. Now, ten years later, comes this new edition—even more complete than the original. It is a triumph not in the least diminished by the tragic passing of Arnie Watson on April 21, 1984. Rather, it becomes a lasting monument to his dedication and scholarship.

This new edition reflects ten years of additional knowledge as to exactly who served on the lost liner, what they did, where they lived, and what became of them. For instance, the Third Class Matron was Mrs. Wallis, not Wallace; G. Chitty was Assistant Baker, not Steward; Fireman W. Barrett lived at 24, not 26 Bevois Street, Southampton. Fireman W. Clark was lost, not saved; while Bedroom Steward T. Clark was saved, not lost; and Fireman Thomas Hart was not on board at all. It's this loving care in getting things right that makes the Watson's list so valuable.

Besides being an indispensable reference tool, the list is a fascinating social document. It tells us so much about the *Titanic* and her era, especially the enormous complexity of the great liners of the period. There were not only sailors, stewards, firemen and such, but linen keepers, window cleaners, confectioners, stenographers, even a Vienna Baker. On the *Titanic* it took a total of nine "Boots" just to keep the passengers' shoes shined!

The list also drives home once again the heroic sacrifice made by the *Titanic's* crew. The band, the bellboys, the engineers,—all lost. Poignant in a different way was the fate of the personnel of the à la carte restaurant. Largely Italian and French, they seem to have had practically no chance at all—only one saved.

On the other hand, there were the lucky ones. A surprising number of the crew, for one reason or another, saved their lives by missing the boat. A total of thirteen men either deserted, or "left by consent", or failed to join just before the *Titanic* sailed on April 10, 1912. Perhaps the luckiest of all were the three Slade brothers. Listed as firemen, all three seemed to have jumped ship at the last moment!

Along with the list, the Watsons have included several articles, giving us a touching glimpse of Halifax immediately following the disaster, plus detailed information helping the visitor to Halifax today. Good plans show the location of the three cemeteries containing the remains of some 150 *Titanic* victims, and the location of particular graves within each cemetery. Every student of the *Titanic* should be grateful for this addition to the canon.

Walter Lord

PREFACE

Many years have gone by since the freezing waters of the North Atlantic closed over the grave of the *Titanic*. Why bother with an alphabetical crew list at this late date? For the reason that it is alphabetical. *Lloyd's List* makes no pretense at any alphabetical arrangement; the names are divided into sixteen categories according to the section of the ship in which the man or woman served.

The U.S. Senate Investigation List is alphabetical but divided into three departments; Deck, Engine and Victualing. In order to use this list one would have to know what the person's job was.

The *Eaton List* is alphabetical by rating and contains no addresses.

This crew list is based on four sources:

The Deathless Story of the Titanic by Sir Philip Gibbs, published by Lloyd's Weekly News, London, 1912.

Congressional Record - Senate - May 28, 1912, pages 7292 to 7300, Exhibit "A", - Particulars of crew of steamship *Titanic* (more commonly known as the *Senate Investigation List*).

A Titanic Crew List compiled and edited by John P. Eaton, August 1967. (Mr. Eaton is historian of The Titanic Historical Society.)

Research (1972) in Halifax, Nova Scotia.

Lloyd's List and *Senate Investigation List* are based on records of the White Star Line and, more directly, on lists prepared while on board the *Carpathia* by Second Officer Charles H. Lightoller ("Deck" and "Engine" Departments, Seamen and Firemen) Chief Second Class Steward John Hardy ("Victualing" Department, Stewards, Cooks, Messmen, etc.)

Lloyd's List was published shortly after the

sinking. It is based on names whose correct spelling might be presumed to have been regarded as less reliable than the *Senate Investigation List* which was prepared about a month after the disaster and under closer supervision. In this list the spelling of the names and the addresses are based on the *Senate Investigation List*, with but few exceptions.

The letter R in brackets (R) to the right of the rating indicates an employee of the Ritz Restaurant. While meals were included in the amount paid for passage, if one wanted to be more exclusive one could take one's meals in the "à la carte" restaurant at fancy prices. This restaurant was located on B Deck (Promenade Deck). Mr. Luigi Gatti, formerly of Oddeninov's Imperial Restaurant, London, was the manager.

As each body was taken out of the sea it was assigned a number; personal effects were put in a bag and given the same number. That number was put on each headstone whether the body was identified or not. The *Mackay-Bennett* brought to Halifax, or buried at sea, numbers 1 to 306, the *Minia* numbers 307 to 323 and the *Montmagny* numbers 324 to 340 with the exception of number 330 which is explained on page 00 of the numerical listing. (Numbers 324 and 325 were unaccounted for.)

While this was a working voyage for Thomas Andrews his official status was that of a passenger. He occupied cabin A36 according to a copy of the first class passenger list. The remaining nine members of the Harland and Wolff guarantee group are listed with the crew but are identified, as such, in the address column.

There were four American Line employees travelling as passengers but living and listed with the crew: Johnson, A.; Johnson, W.; Leonard, L.; Turnguist, W. Only Mr. Turnguist survived.

THE TITANIC - HALIFAX STORY

by *Arnold Watson*
with *Elizabeth L. Watson*

In 1898, a struggling author named Morgan Robertson wrote a book about a fabulous Atlantic liner far larger than anything then in existence. He named his fictional ship *Titan*, and sent her across the north Atlantic. On a cold April night she raced ahead, heedless of iceberg warnings, struck a berg, and went down carrying the rich and complacent to the bottom with her. Robertson called his story, *Futility*.

On June 20th of that same year, my father and mother were married. They spent part of their honeymoon in New York City. In this day and age, there were no bridges across the Hudson nor tunnels under it. Passengers going into New York had to end their rail journey at Jersey City, New Jersey, and take a ferry-boat across the Hudson to Manhattan. To those who can remember the ferry-boat of that period, the passengers sat with their backs to the water facing the horses and wagons that were in the center of the ferry. My mother was seated in just such a position. A little boy alongside her was kneeling on the seat and looking out the window. He excitedly shouted, "There goes the *La Bourgogne!*"

My mother turned and looked out the window and saw this beautiful white French liner going out of New York Harbor. That was the last that New Yorkers or anyone was to see of the *La Bourgogne.* July 4th she collided with the British sailing vessel, *Cromartyshire* in a fog and went down off Sable Island with the loss of 584 persons. As in the case of the *Titanic*, the city of Halifax responded with men and ships to the scene of the sinking.

1

In the many books on my shelves dealing with
the wreck of the *Titanic*, only five of them touch on
the part that the city of Halifax, the *Mackay—
Bennett*, the *Minia*, and the *Montmagny* played in it.
None of these are mentioned to any great degree.
Sinking Of The Titanic by Jay Henry Mowbray,
Ph.d.; LL.D. (1912) devotes one short chapter to the
gathering of the dead. *Sinking Of The Titanic* by
Logan Marshall (1912) gives even a smaller amount
of space to this aspect of the wreck. *Tramps And
Ladies*, by Sir James Bisset, dismisses the part
played by the *Mackay-Bennett* with one short para-
graph. Peter Padfield, in his book, *The Titanic And
The Californian*, gives the work that the *Mackay-
Bennett* did in six sentences. John Maxtone-
Graham, in his magnificent work, *The Only Way To
Cross*, gives it one and one-fourth pages.

In the summer of 1971, my wife and I fulfilled a
desire of long-standing by visiting the Maritime
Provinces of Canada. We sailed from New York on
the German-Atlantic cruise ship *Hamburg*. Our last
port of call in Canada was Halifax; a city of 123,000
serving a metropolitan area of 206,000.

Most people remember Halifax because of the
great explosion that took place on December 17,
1917; the collision of two ships, the *Mont Blanc*
carrying T.N.T. and the *Imo* which was a ship carrying supplies to the relief of the Belgians. It resulted
in the largest man-made explosion prior to the
atomic bomb, causing $50,000,000 in property dam-
age, 2,000 deaths and 8,000 injured.

Few, if any, will remember the part this city
played in the gathering up and interring the dead
from the *Titanic* disaster. Our cruise ship was only
in the harbor one day and we took one of the sight-
seeing tours. During the tour, our guide mentioned
that there were three cemeteries in the city in which

the victims of the *Titanic* were buried. I picked up my ears and asked the guide to give me the names of the three cemeteries, making a firm resolve to come back sometime in the future and investigate them.

In the summer of 1972, Mrs. Watson and I flew to Halifax and spent a very memorable week there, photographing the burial plots and individual headstones in the three cemeteries. I visited the Halifax library and it had some information on the *Titanic,* including Charles Lightoller's book, *Titanic And Other Ships.*

Later, we visited the Public Archives of Nova Scotia where most of our time from then on was spent in the Archives where the people were most kind in allowing my wife to photograph whatever we wanted and in supplying me with the dry copies of newspapers, passenger lists, etc.

Cable ship *Mackay-Bennett* in a peaceful cove off the coast of Nova Scotia circa 1910

Close-up of the long piece of oak. Note the intricate design of the carving.

A long piece of carved oak with musical motif, also brought in by the *Minia.*

A large piece of carved oak with musical motif, also brought in by the *Minia.*

Photos courtesy Elizabeth L. Watson

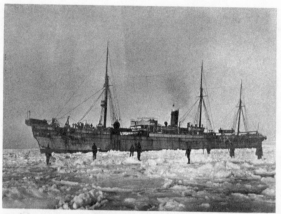

Cable Ship *Minia* in the ice.

CGS Montmagny, a lighthouse supply and bouy tender.

A body from the *Ti-tanic* being pulled out of the sea.

Photos of Minia and body being pulled from the sea were furnished by the Public Archives of Nova Scotia. The Photo of the *CGS Montmagny* was furnished by Thomas E. Appleton, Historian, Marine Administration, Ministry of Transport, Ottawa.

AFTERMATH OF A TRAGEDY

The cable ship *Mackay-Bennett* which had been sent out to recover as many as possible of the *Titanic's* dead, reached her pier in the dockyard at Halifax, Nova Scotia, the nearest port, at 9:30 on the morning of April 30, almost exactly two weeks after the disaster.

Down the gangway to the pier in the sunlight of a perfect April day they carried 190 of those who had started forth on the maiden voyage of the biggest ship afloat.

In her quest the *Mackay-Bennett* had found 306 of the *Titanic's* dead, but only 190 were brought to shore. The rest, the 116, were buried at sea.

The search was continued over five days, sometimes with the ship drifting without success amid miles and miles of wreckage, tables, chairs, doors, pillows, scattered fragments of the luxury that was the White Star liner *Titanic*.

At other times the bodies were found close together, and once they saw more than a hundred that looked to the wondering crew of the *Mackay-Bennett* like a flock of sea gulls in the fog, so strangely did the ends of the life belts rise and fall with the waves.

It was a little after 9:30 that the *Mackay-Bennett* was sighted by those waiting for her since the break of day. For it was in the chill of 6 o'clock on a Canadian Spring morning that the people began to assemble on the pier in the dockyard.

They were undertakers for the most part, mingling with the newspaper men who hurried to and fro between the water's edge and the little bell tent set up a few yards back to guard the wires that were to flash the news to the ends of the continent.

The dockyard was patrolled by twenty members of the crew and four petty officers from *H. M. C. S. Niobe* and by a squad of men from the Dominion police, who were instructed to keep out all without passes countersigned by the commandant, and who were particularly vigilant in the watch for men with cameras.

Just as the death ship reached her pier, and in the midst of the eager movement forward to learn what news she brought from the scene of the *Titanic's* wreck, a little tug was spotted nearby, and Commander Martin, in charge of the dockyard, scented a moving picture man.

In a very few moments he was putting out for the tug in the little patrol launch. Again a few moments and he was standing on the pier with a complacent smile on his face.

"I have the films," he said in explanation, so the privacy was guarded.

Then, warned by the tolling of the bells up in the town, a hush fell upon the waiting people. The gray clouds that had overcast the sky parted, and the sun shone brilliantly on the rippling water of the harbor as the *Mackay-Bennett* drew alongside her pier.

Captain Lardner could be seen upon the bridge. The crew hung over the sides, joyously alive and glad to be home. But in every part of the ship the dead lay. High on the poop deck coffins and rough shells were piled and piled.

Dead men in tarpaulins lined the flooring of the cable-wells both fore and aft, so that there was hardly room for a foot to be put down. And in the forward hold dead men were piled one upon another, their eyes closed as in sleep, and over them all a great tarpaulin was stretched. Those that pressed forward to see were sickened and turned back.

The uncoffined dead were carried down in stretchers, placed in the rough shells that were piled upon the pier, and one by one driven up the slope and into the town in the long line of hearses and black undertaker's wagons that had been gathered from every quarter. It was speedily done, but quietly and without irreverent haste.

For two hours this business proceeded before anyone could go upon the pier and the sounds were like the hum of a small factory. There were the muffled orders, the shuffling and tramping of feet, the scraping as of packing boxes drawn across the rough flooring and the eternal hammering that echoed all along the coal sheds.

Two hours it was before anyone could go on *Titanic*'s crew, but the slender hope that their own were swung down from the deck and piled up on the wharf ready for the removal that took until well into the middle of the afternoon.

At the Mayflower Curling Rink at the edge of

the town, the line of hearses had been trundling since the *Mackay-Bennett* landed. As they passed the crowds were hushed, men bowed their heads, and officers saluted.

Of those who were brought to shore, 60 lay unnamed at the curling rink on the edge of the town. It was believed that the 60 were all members of the *Titanic's* crew, but the slender hope that their own dead might be among them sent many to the rink.

One of the 60 was a little baby boy (the only child's body to be recovered). Five of them were women, but none of the women that were found were from the first cabin passengers. The quest of the *Mackay-Bennett* bore greater results than were anticipated, and Capt. Lardner believed that his ship recovered about all of those who did not go down in the *Titanic*.

The hallway of the curling rink where the dead were removed from the cable ship was thronged all afternoon with friends and relatives eager beyond expression to see those unnamed dead, but the attention of the embalmers was turned to those already identified, for whom the claimants were waiting. For the most part of the unidentified could not be viewed until the next morning.

The suspense was acute. Yet those who were most anxious for the morrow to come knew that hope was of the slenderest. They knew that the nameless sixty were almost all members of the crew. Capt. Lardner said that he was sure of it. He knew it by the clothes they wore.

Upstairs in the large, bare room the packets of clothing were distributed in rows upon the floor.

There the oak chests of the Provincial Cashier were opened for the sorting of the canvas bags that contained the valuables, the letters and the identifying trinkets of the dead. It was all very systematic.

It was all very much businesslike, and while a lunch counter served refreshments to the weary workers, and while the Intercolonial set up a desk for railway tickets, the Medical Examiner was busy issuing death certificates, and the Registrar was issuing burial permits, all to the accompanying click, click of several typewriters.

A satisfactory arrangement was reached as to the disposition of the personal effects. A man would claim his dead, take the number, make his way to the representatives of the Provincial Secretary, and there claim the contents of the little canvas bag by making affidavit that he was the duly authorized representative of the executor or next of kin.

The little crimson tickets that are the death certificates were printed for the tragedies of every day in the year. Their formal points and dimensions seemed hopelessly inadequate for even the briefest statement of the tragedy of the *Titanic*.

The first body claimed and removed from the rink was that of John Jacob Astor. The certificate, the first issued for one of the *Titanic* dead, reads:

Name of deceased—John Jacob Astor. Sex—M. Age—47. Date of death—April 15, 1912. Residence, street, etc.—840 Fifth Av., N. Y. C. Occupation— Gentleman. Married. Cause—Accidental drowning. *S. S. Titanic* at sea. Length of illness—Suddenly. Name of physician in attendance.

After the greater part of the *Titanic's* dead had been shifted from the *Mackay-Bennett* to the pier, Captain Lardner descended to the dining saloon, and with the reporters from all over the country gathered around the table, he opened the ship's log and, slowly tracing his fingers over the terse entries, he told them the story of the death ship's voyage.

Lardner is English by birth and accent, and tall

and square of build, with a full brown beard and eyes of unusual keenness.

"Let me say first of all," he announced when the reporters gathered around him, "that I was commissioned to bring aboard all the bodies found floating, but owing to the unanticipated number of bodies found, owing to the bad weather and other conditions it was impossible to carry out instructions, so some were committed to the deep after service, conducted by Canon Hind."

"We left Halifax," he continued, "shortly after noon on Wednesday, April 17, but fog and bad weather delayed us on the run out, and we did not get there till Saturday night at 8 o'clock.

"We asked all ships to report to us if they passed any wreckage or bodies, and on Saturday at noon we received a communication from the German mailboat steamship *Rhein* to the effect that in latitude 42.1. N. longitude 49.13, she had passed wreckage and bodies.

"The course was shaped for that position. Later in the afternoon we spoke to the German steamship *Bremen*, and they reported having passed three large icebergs and some bodies in 42 N. 49.20 W.

"We arrived on the scene at 8 o'clock Saturday evening, and then we stopped and let the ship drift. It was in the middle of the watch that some of the wreckage and a few bodies were sighted.

"At daylight the boats were lowered, and though there was a heavy sea running at the time, fifty-one bodies were recovered."

The Rev. Canon K. C. Hinds, rector of All Saints' Cathedral, who officiated at the burial of 116 bodies, the greatest number consigned to the ocean at one time, tells the story of the *Mackay-Bennett's* trip as follows:

We left Halifax shortly after noon on April 17, and had not proceeded far when fog set in so that our journey was slow. We reached the vicinity of the wreckage on Saturday evening. Early on Sunday morning the search for bodies began, when the captain and other officers of the ship kept a lookout from the bridge.

Soon the command was given "Stand by the boat!" and a little later the lifeboat was lowered and the work begun of picking up the bodies as they were pointed out in the water to the crew.

Through the day some fifty were picked up. All were carefully examined and their effects placed in separate bags, all bodies and bags being numbered.

It was deemed wise that some of them should be buried. At 8 P. M. the ship's bell was tolled to indicate all was in readiness for the service. Standing on the bow of the ship as she rocked to and fro, one gazed at the starry heavens and across the boundless deep, and to his mind the psalmist's words came with mighty force.

"Whither shall I go then from Thy spirit, or whither shall I go then from Thy presence? If I ascend up to heaven Thou art there, I make my bed in the grave, Thou art there also. If I take the wings of the morning and dwell in the uttermost part of the sea, even there shall Thy hand lead me, and Thy right hand shall hold me."

In the solemn stillness of the early night, the words of that unequaled burial office rang across the waters: "I am the resurrection and the life, saith the Lord. He that believeth in Me shall never die."

When the time of committal came these words were used over each body:

"Forasmuch as it hath pleased Almighty God to take upto Himself the soul of our dear brother departed, we, therefore, commit his body to the deep to be turned to corruption, looking for the resurrection of the body (when the seas shall give up her dead) and the life of the world to come, through Jesus Christ Our Lord, who shall change our vile body, that it may be like unto His glorious body, according to the mighty working whereby He is able to subdue all things to Himself."

The prayers from the burial service were said, the hymn "Jesus, Lover of My Soul," sung and the blessing given.

Any one attending a burial at sea will most surely lose the common impression of the awfulness of a grave in the mighty deep. The wild Atlantic may rage and toss, the shipwrecked mariners cry for mercy, but far below in the calm untroubled depth they rest in peace.

On Monday the work began again early in the morning, and another day was spent in searching and picking up the floating bodies and at night a number were buried. On Tuesday the work was still the same until the afternoon, when the fog set in, and continued all day Wednesday.

Wednesday was partly spent in examining bodies, and at noon a number were committed to the deep. Thursday came in fine and from early morning until evening the work went on.

During the day word came that the cable ship Minia was on her way to help and would be near us at midnight.

"Early on Friday some more bodies were picked up. The captain then felt we had covered the ground fairly well and decided to start on our homeward way at noon. After receiving some supplies from the Minia we bid good-bye and proceeded on our way.

"The Mackay-Bennett succeeded in finding 306 bodies, of which 116 were buried at sea, and one could not help feeling, as we steamed homeward, that of those bodies we had on board it would be well if the greater number of them were resting in the deep.

"It is to be noted how earnestly and reverently all the work was done and how nobly the crew acquitted themselves during a work of several days which meant a hard and trying strain on mind and body.

"What seems a very regrettable fact is that in chartering the *Mackay-Bennett* for this work the White Star Company did not send an official agent to accompany the steamer in her search for the bodies," Canon Hinds concluded.

—from *Sinking of the Titanic*, by Jay Henry Mowbray. Published in 1912 by The Minter Company, Harrisburg, Pa. Edited by John P. Eaton and Charles A. Haas, Titanic Historical Society, 1984.

Titanic Crew List

The names of the survivors are in CAPITOL LETTERS. Unless otherwise stated all addresses are Southampton.

NAME	ADDRESS	RATING	NUMBER
Abbot, E.	98 Northumberland Rd.	Pantryman (Lounge)	
Abrams, C.	3 Charles St.	Fireman	
Adams, R.	168 Romsey Rd.	Fireman	
Ahier, P.	136 Northumberland Rd.	Saloon Steward	
Akerman, A.	25 Rochester St.	Steward	
Akerman, J.	25 Rochester St.	Asst. Pantryman	205
Allaria, Baptiste	9 Orchard Place	Asst. Waiter (R)	221
Allen, G.	32 Grove St.	Scullion	
ALLEN, E.	9 Short St.	Trimmer	
Allen, F.	Short St.	Lift Attendent	
Allen, Henry	3 French St.	Fireman	145
Allen, R.	Charlton Rd., Shirley	Bedroom Steward	
Allsop, F.	73 Obelisk Rd., Woolston	Saloon Steward	
Alsopp, Alfred Samuel	134 Malmesbury Rd.	Jr. Electrician	
ANDERSON, J.	1 Couzens Court	Able Seaman	
Anderson, Walter J.	12 Queen's Terrace	Bedroom Steward	146
ANDREWS, C. E.	145 Millbrook Rd.	Officers Steward	

17

NAME	ADDRESS	RATING	NUMBER
ARCHER, ERNEST	59 Porchester Rd.	Able Seaman	
Ashe, H. W.	15 Wyresdale Rd., Liverpool	G. H. Steward	34
Ashcroft, A.	28 Canterbury Rd., Seacombe, Cheshire	Clerk	
Aspilagi, George	79 St. Paul's Rd., London	Asst. Plateman (R)	
AVERY, J.	122 Hills Rd.	Trimmer	
Ayling, G.	22 Wilton St.	Asst. Vegetable Cook	
Back, C. F.	38 Weymouth Terrace	Asst. Lounge Steward	
Bagley, E.	183 Priory Rd.	Saloon Steward	
BAGGOTT, A. M.	106 Park Rd., Freemantle, Southampton	Saloon Steward	
Bailey, G. F.	Brooklands, Shepperton	Saloon Steward	161
BAILEY, HENRY	377 Portswood Road	Master-At-Arms	
Bailey, G. W.	16 Brook St., Woolston	Fireman	
Baines, Richard	9 Union Place	Greaser	
BALL, PERCY	7 Windsor Terrace	Platewasher	
Ball, W.	51 Brintons Rd.	Fireman	
Banfi, Ugo	33 Aubert Park Highbury Hill,	Waiter (R)	
Bannon, J.	9 St. George's Street	Greaser	
Barker, H.	Kingsworthy, Winchester	Asst. Baker	

NAME	ADDRESS	RATING	NUMBER
Barker, Ernest T.	4 Grand Parade, Harringay	Saloon Steward	159
Barker, R. L.	Maybush, Old Shirley	2nd Purser	
Barker, T.	20 Upper Bugle Street	Asst. Butcher	
Barlow, C.	10 St. Mary's Road	Fireman	
Barlow, G.	Foundry Lane	Bedroom Steward	
Barnes, Charles	45 York Rd.	Fireman	
Barnes, F.	25 Parsonage Road	Asst. Baker	
Barnes, J.	Woodley Rd., Woolston	Fireman	
Barrett, A.	164 North-umberland Rd.	Bell Boy	
BARRETT, FREDERICK	24 King St.	Leading Fireman	
Barrett, W.	24 Bevois St.	Fireman	
Barringer, A.W.	52 Padwell Rd.	Saloon Steward	
Barrow, H.	17 Derby Rd.	Asst. Butcher	
Barrows, William	34 Hanover St., Islington, London	Saloon Steward	
Barton, S. J.	85 College St.	Steward	
Basilico, Giovanni	27 Old Compton St., London	Waiter (R)	
Baxter, H. R.	110 Shirley Rd.	Bedroom Steward	
Baxter, Thomas F.	81 Atherley Rd.	Linen Keeper	235

NAME	ADDRESS	RATING	NUMBER
Bazzi, Narcisso	21 Great Chapel St., London	Waiter (R)	
Beattie, F.	3 Isthmus St., Belfast	Greaser	
BEAUCHAMP, GEORGE, W.	Redbridge Rd.	Fireman	
Beedem, G.	81 Shrewsbury Rd., Harlesden	Bedroom Steward	
Beere, Wm.	2 Avenue Cottage, Shirley	Kitchen Porter	
Belford, Walter	163 Manor Rd., Itchen	Chief Night Baker	
Bell, William Joseph	34 Canute Rd.	Chief Engineer	
Bellows, J.	28 Bell St.	Trimmer	
Bendell, T.	26 Woodley Rd.	Fireman	
Benham, F.	61 Peach St. Wokingham	Saloon Steward	
Bennett, G.	3 Deal St.	Fireman	
BENNETT, MRS. M.	29 Cranbury Avenue	Stewardess	
Bernardi, Baptiste	113 High St., Nottinghill Gate, London	Asst. Waiter (R)	215
Benville, E.	4 Orchard Lane	Fireman	
Bessant, E.	39 Shirley Park Rd.	Baggage Steward	
Bessant, W.	36 Henry Rd.	Fireman	
Best, E.	87 Malmesbury Road	Saloon Steward	
Beaux, David	5 Beauchamp Place, London	Asst. Waiter (R)	

NAME	ADDRESS	RATING	NUMBER
Bevis, J.	171 Empress Road	Trimmer	
Bietrix, G.	22 Albert Mansions, London	Sauce Cook (R)	
Biddlecomb, C.	42 Kentish Rd.	Fireman	
Biggs, E.	65 College St.	Fireman	
BINSTEAD, W.	49 Endle St.	Trimmer	
Bishop, W.	17 High Street, Itchen	Bedroom Steward	
Black, A.	6 Briton St.	Fireman	
Black, D.	Sailor's Home, Southampton	Fireman	
Blackman, H.	58 College St.	Fireman	
BLAKE, P.	18 Endle St.	Trimmer	
Blake, S.	Holyrood House	Mess Steward Engine Dept.	
Blake, T.	35 Peel St., Northam	Fireman	
Blaney, J.	Sailor's Home, Southampton	Fireman	
Blann, E.	99 Pound St.	Fireman	
BLISS, MISS E.	56 Upper Park Rd., New Southgate	Stewardess	
Blumet, Jean	26 Richmond Street	Plateman (R)	
Bogie, L.	100 Crescent, Eastleigh	Bedroom Steward	274
Bochetez, J.	28 Oakbank Rd.	Asst. Chef	
Bollin, Henri	37 Orchard Place	Larder Cook (R)	
Bond, W.	20 Hanley Rd.	Bedroom Steward	

22

NAME	ADDRESS	RATING	NUMBER
Boothby, W.	31 Winchester Rd., Shirley	Bedroom Steward	107
Boston, W.	1 Hanley Rd.	Asst. Deck Steward	
Bott, W.	6 Nichols Rd.	Greaser	
Bouchet, Giuseppi	Mercer St., London	Second Head Waiter (R)	
Boughton, B.	10 Richmond Rd.	Saloon Steward	
BOWKER, MISS R.	The Cottage, Little Sutton, Cheshire	First Cashier (R)	
*BOXHALL, JOSEPH GROVE	Westbourne Ave., Hull	4th Officer	
Boyd, J.	52 Cranbury Avenue	Saloon Steward	
Boyes, J. H.	106 Clovelly Road	Saloon Steward	
Bradley, F.	25 Threefield Lane	Able Seaman	
Bradley, P.	4 Green's Court	Fireman	
Bradshaw, J. A.	2 Portland St.	Platewasher	
Brailey, Theodore	71 Lancaster Rd., Ladbroke Grove, London	Orchestra (Pianist)	
Brewer, H.	27 Palmerston Road	Trimmer (Deserted 4/10/12)	
Brewster, G. H.	5 Carlton Place	Bedroom Steward	
BRICE, W.	11 Lower Canal Walk	Able Seaman	

*Last surviving officer of the TITANIC. His remains were scattered on the sea June 12, 1967 over the position where the wreck lies.

NAME	ADDRESS	RATING	NUMBER
Bricoux, Roger	Place Du Lion D'or Lille, France	Orchestra (Cellist)	
BRIDE, HAROLD S.	Bannister's Hotel	Jr. Marconi Operator	
BRIGHT, ARTHUR JOHN	105 Firgrove Road	Quartermaster	
Bristow, H.	Shortlands, Kent	Saloon Steward	
Bristow, R. C.	49 West Ridge Rd.	Steward	290
Brookman, J.	34 Richmond Street	Steward	
Brooks, J.	128 Lyons St.	Trimmer	
Broome, Athol T.	White Lodge Bitterne Park	Asst. Veranda Cafe Steward	
Broom, H.	2 High St., East Cowes	Bath Steward	
BROWN, EDWARD	43 Suffolk Rd.	Saloon Steward	
Brown, J.	237 Desborough Rd., Eastleigh	Fireman	
Brown, J.	2 Russell St.	Fireman	267
Brown, W.	Hillside Ave.	Saloon Steward	
Brugge, W.	Sailor's Home, Southampton	Fireman	
Burton, H.	St. Andrew's Road	Steward	
Buckley, H.	7 Brunswick Square	Asst. Vegetable Cook	
BULEY, EDWARD JOHN	10 Cliff Rd., Woolston	Able Seaman	
Bull, W.	27 Chandall St.	Scullion	

24

NAME	ADDRESS	RATING	NUMBER
Bulley, H.	31 Carleton Crescent	Boots	
Bunnell, W.	212 Bedford Rd., Liverpool	Plate Washer	
*BURGESS, CHARLES	65 Bridge Rd.	Extra 3rd Baker	
Burke, R. E.	26 Southampton Road, Chandlersford	Lounge Attendant	
BURKE, WILLIAM	57 Bridge Road	Second Saloon Steward	
Burr, E.	34 Victoria Rd., Woolston, Hants	Saloon Steward	
BURRAGE, A.	9 Emsworth Rd.	Plates	
Burroughs, A.	73 Adelaide Rd.	Fireman	
Burrows, W.	Elm St.	Fireman (Left by consent 4/10/12)	
Burton, E.	24 Chapel St.	Fireman	
Butt, R.	6 Cawte Rd.	Saloon Steward	10
Butt, W.	6 Cawte Rd.	Fireman	77
Butterworth, J.	270 Priory Rd.	Saloon Steward	116
Byrne, J.	218 Balfour Rd., Ilford, Essex	Bedroom Steward	
Calderwood, H.	Sailor's Home, Southampton	Trimmer	
Campbell, Donald S.	White Star Line	Clerk (Kitchen)	
Campbell, William	Employee of Harland & Wolff Belfast	Joiner Apprentice	

*Last Titanic crewman on active sea service.

NAME	ADDRESS	RATING	NUMBER
Carney, William	11 Cairo St., West Derby Rd., Liverpool	Lift Attendant	251
Carr, R.	Welham Cottage, Winchester Rd.	Trimmer	
Cartwright, James Edward	77 Gossett St., London	Saloon Steward	320
Casali, Guido	50 Greek St., Soho, London	Waiter (R)	
Casey, T.	Sailor's Home, Southampton	Trimmer	
Casswill, C.	81 Melbourne Street	Saloon Steward	
Castleman, E.	37 North Rd., St. Deny's	Greaser	
CATON, MISS A.	50 Highbury Hill, London	Turkish Bath Attendant	
Caunt, W.	55 Sidney Rd.	Grill Cook	
Cave, Herbert	17 Shirley Park Rd., London	Saloon Steward	218
CAVELL, GEORGE	Lower East Rd., Sholing	Trimmer	
Cecil, C.	194 Millbrook Road	Steward	
CHAPMAN, J.	31 Bellevue Road	Boots	
Charboisson, Adrian	19 Kensington Park Gardens, London	Roast Cook (R)	
Charman, John	Malden Hill House, Lewisham	Saloon Steward	
Cherrett, W.	13 Nelson Rd.	Fireman	

NAME	ADDRESS	RATING	NUMBER
Cheverton, W.	Mile St., Newport I.O.W.	Saloon Steward	
Chisolm, Roderick	Employee of Harland & Wolff, Belfast	Ship's Draughts-man (Designed Titanic's Life-boats)	
Chiswall, George Alexander	53 High St., Itchen	Sr. Boiler Maker	111
Chitty, G.	Newtown Rd., Bitterne	Asst. Baker	
*Chiverton, W. F.	Mill St., Newport	Saloon Steward	
Chorley, J.	2 Regent St.	Fireman	
Christmas, H.	4 Brintons Rd.	Asst. Steward	
CLARK, T.	Hillside Ave.	Bedroom Steward	
Clarke, J. Fred	22 Tunstall St., Smithdown Rd., Liverpool	Orchestra (Bass)	202
Clark, W.	30 Paget St.	Fireman	
CLENCH, FREDERICK	Chantry Rd.	Able Seaman	
Clench, G.	Chantry Rd.	Able Seaman	
Coe, H.	10 Cross Court	Trimmer	
**COFFEY, JOHN	Sperbourne Terrace	Fireman	
Coleman, A.	Oaktree Rd.	Saloon Steward	
Coleman, John	7 Mortimer Rd., Itchen	Mess Steward, Engine Dept.	
COLGAN, JOSEPH	27 West St.	Scullion	

*Body found on June 8, 1912 at 49.06 N., 42.51 W., by ship ILFORD. Recommitted to the deep.
**Deserted at Queenstown.

NAME	ADDRESS	RATING	NUMBER
COLLINS, JOHN	65 Ballycarry Rd., Belfast	Scullion	
COLLINS, SAMUEL	Sailor's Home, Southampton	Fireman	
Conner, J.	17 Shamrock Rd., Woolston	Fireman	
Conraire, Morel	15 Trafalgar Square, London	Asst. Roast Cook (R)	
Contin, Augusto	37 Orchard Pl.	Entree Cook (R)	
Conway, P. W.	25 South Front, Hackney	Saloon Steward	
Cook, C.	Chantry Rd.	Steward	
Cook, George	13 Franklin Rd.	Saloon Steward	
COOMBES, G.	45 Coleman St.	Fireman	
Coombs, C.	78 Dykes Rd.	Asst. Cook	
Cooper, H.	9 St. George's Street	Fireman	
Cooper, J.	27 Pound St.	Trimmer	
Copper-thwaite, B.	39 Mount St.	Fireman	
Corben, E. T.	58 Floating Bridge Road	Asst. Printer	
Corcoran, D.	Sailor's Home, Southampton	Fireman	
Cotton, A.	Shore Cottages, Hythe	Fireman	
Couch, F.	Port Isaac, Cornwall	Able Seaman	
Couch, J.	42 Canton St.	Greaser	
COUPER, R.	101 Duke St.	Fireman	
Cox, Will Denton	110 Shirley Rd.	Steward	300
Coy, Francis Edward George	134 Porstwood Road	Jr. 3rd Asst. Engineer	

NAME	ADDRESS	RATING	NUMBER
Crabb, H.	101 Firgrove Road	Trimmer	
CRAFTER, F.	143 Albert Rd.	Saloon Steward	
CRAWFORD, ALFRED	22 Cranbury Avenue	Bedroom Steward	
Creese, Henry Philip	2 Enfield Grove, Woolston	Deck Engineer	
CRIMMINS, J.	7 King Street	Fireman	
Crisp, H.	36 Macnaughten Road	Saloon Steward	
Crispin, William	Sanfoin Villa, Eastleigh	G.H. Steward	
Crosbie, J. B.	47 St. Dunstan's Road, London	Turkish Bath Attendant	
Cross, W.	97 Ludlow Rd.	Fireman	
Crovelle, Louis	5 Orchard Place	Asst. Waiter (R)	
CROWE, GEORGE FREDERICK	89 Milton Rd.	Saloon Steward	
Crumplin, Charles	Anchor & Hope, Threefield Lane	Bedroom Steward	
CULLEN, CHARLES	24 Warberton Rd., Liverpool	Bedroom Steward	
Cunningham, Alfred	Employee of Harland & Wolff Belfast	Fitter Apprentice	
CUNNINGHAM, ANDREW	60 Charlton Rd.	Bedroom Steward	
Cunningham, B.	6 Briton St.	Fireman	
Curtis, A.	55 Kingsley Rd.	Fireman	
DANIELS, SIDNEY E.	119 Albert Rd., South Sea	Steward	

NAME	ADDRESS	RATING	NUMBER
Dashwood, Will G.	Sailor's Home, Southampton	Saloon Steward	83
Davies, Gordon	Hillside Ave.	Bedroom Steward	
Davies, J. J.	19 Eastfield Rd.	Extra 2nd Baker	200
Davies, R. J.	12 The Polygon Road	Saloon Steward	
Davies, T.	2 Church Lane	Leading Fireman	
Davis, Stephen J.	42 Duncan St., Landport	Able Seaman	
Dawes, W. W.	Nelson Rd.	Steward (Discharged 4/10/12)	
Dawson, J.	70 Briton St.	Trimmer	227
Dean, George H.	King Edward Ave., London	Asst. Steward	252
Debreuca, Maurice	12 Meade St., London	Asst. Waiter (R)	244
Deeble, Alfred	81 Atherley Rd.	Saloon Steward	270
Denarcissio, ---	20 Church St., Soho, London	Asst. Waiter (R)	
Deslands, Percy	405 Portswood Road	Saloon Steward	212
Derrett, A.	Hillside Ave.	Saloon Steward	
Desornini, Louis	4 Queen's Park Terrace	Asst. Pastry Cook (R)	
DIAPER, J.	102 Derby Rd.	Fireman	
Dickson, W.	10 Oriental Terrace	Trimmer	
DILLEY, J.	44 Threefield Lane	Fireman	
DILLON, THOMAS PATRICK	Sailor's Home, Southampton	Trimmer	

NAME	ADDRESS	RATING	NUMBER
DiMartino, Giovanni	c/o Gatti	Asst. Waiter (R)	
Dimenage, J. K.	4 Cawte Rd.	Saloon Steward	
Dodd, Edward C.	26 Queen's Parade	Jr. 3rd Engineer	
Dodd, George	57 Morris Rd.	Chief Second Steward	
Dodds, Renny Watson	12 Queen's Park Terrace	Jr. 4th Asst. Engineer	
DOEL, F.	20 Richmond Street	Fireman	
Dolby, Joseph	12 Devonshire Road	Reception Room Attendant	
Donati, Italo	3 Whitefield St., Tottenham Court Rd., London	Asst. Waiter (R)	311
Donoghue, T.	60 Ludlow Rd.	Bedroom Steward	
DORE, A.	9 Mount St.	Trimmer	
Dornier, Louis	3 Orchard Place	Asst. Fish Cook (R)	
Doughty, N.	30 Queen Sq. London	Saloon Steward	
Doyle, L.	10 Orchard Place	Fireman	
Dubb, A.	81 Atherly Rd.	Steward	
Duffy, William	11 Garton Rd., Itchen	Clerk (Engineer Dept.)	
Dunford, W.	16 Bridge St.	Hospital Steward	
Dyer, Henry Ryland	53 Middle St.	Senior Asst. 4th Engineer	
Dyer, W.	46 Stafford Rd.	Saloon Steward	

NAME	ADDRESS	RATING	NUMBER
DYMOND, F.	2 Farmer's Court	Fireman	
Eagle, A. J.	13 Lyon St.	Trimmer	
Eastman, C.	17 Cecil Ave.	Greaser	
EDBROOKE, F.	99 Lake Rd., Landport	Steward	
Ede, G. B.	Manor Farm Road	Steward	
Edge, T. W.	28 Clovelly Rd., Woolston	Deck Steward	
Edwards, C.	7 Brunswick Square	Asst. Pantryman	
Egg, W. H.	1-A Trent Rd., Brixton, London	Steward	
Elliott, Everett Edward	11 Wilmington St., London	Trimmer	317
ELLIS, J. R.	40 Dukes Rd.	Asst. Vegetable Cook	
Ennis, W.	141 Bedford Rd. Southport	Turkish Bath Attendant	
Ervine, Albert	Maryfield, Belfast	Asst. Electrician	
ETCHES, HENRY SAMUEL	23-A Gordon Ave.	Bedroom Steward	
EVANS, ALFRED FRANK	20 Deal St.	Look-Out-Man	
EVANS, FRANK OLIVER	14 Bond St.	Able Seaman	
Evans, George	2 Nightingale Gardens	Steward	
Evans, George	46 Richmond Road	Saloon Steward	

NAME	ADDRESS	RATING	NUMBER
Evans, W.	11 Ryde Terrace, Itchen	Trimmer	
Fairall, H.	31 Surrey St., Ryde, I.O.W.	Saloon Steward	
Farenden, E.	23 South St., Emsworth	Confectioner	
Farquharson, W. E.	94 Wilton Ave.	Senior 2nd Engineer	
FAULKNER, WILLIAM STEPHEN	16 Malmesbury Road	Bedroom Steward	
Fay, F.	31 Stamford St.	Greaser	
Fei, Carlo	26 Anne's Court London	Sculleryman (R)	
Fellowes, A.	51 Bridge Rd.	Asst. Boots	138
Feltham, G.	64 St. Deny's Road	Vienna Baker	
Fenton, F.	19 Middle Rd., Sholing, Hants	Saloon Steward	
Ferrary, Auto	38 St. Mary's Place	Trimmer	
Ferris, W.	5 Hanover Buildings	Leading Fireman	
Finch, H.	32 French St.	Steward	
FITZPATRICK, C.W.N.	93 Millbrook Road	Mess Steward, Engine Dept.	
Fitzpatrick, H.	169 Nelson St., Belfast	Junior Boiler Maker	
FLARTY, E.	21 Stamford St.	Fireman	
FLEET, FREDERICK	9 Norman Rd.	Look-Out-Man	
Fletcher, P. W.	13 Strathville Rd., South-fields, London	Ship's Bugler	

NAME	ADDRESS	RATING	NUMBER
FOLEY, JACK	2 Queen's Rd.	Storekeeper	
FOLEY, W. C.	15 Monsons Rd.	Steward	
Ford, E.	100 Brintons Rd.	Steward	
Ford, F.	66 Oxford St.	Bedroom Steward	
Ford, H.	Royal Oak	Trimmer	
Ford, Thomas	36 Russell St., Liverpool	Leading Fireman	
FORWARD, J.	Sailor's Home, Southampton	Able Seaman	
Foster, A.	38 North Front	Storekeeper	
Fox, W. T.	Polhawn, Springfield Rd., Ealing	Steward	
Franklin, Alan	Egremont, Newton Rd.	Saloon Steward	262
Fraser, James	54 Tennyson Road	Jr. Asst. 3rd Engineer	
Fraser, J.	Sailor's Home, Southampton	Fireman	
FREDERICKS, W.	6 Elm Rd., Chapel	Trimmer	
Freeman, Ernest Edward Samuel	5 Hanley Rd.	Chief Deck Steward*	239
FROPPER, R. P.	8 Washington Terrace	Saloon Steward	
Frost, Anthony W.	Employee of Harland & Wolff Belfast	Outside Foreman Engineer	

*On crew list as Chief Deck Steward, but actually J. Bruce Ismay's secretary.

NAME	ADDRESS	RATING	NUMBER
Frost, Archie	Employee of Harland & Wolff Belfast	Head of Guarantee Group	
FRYER, A.	1 Charlotte Place	Trimmer	
Gallop, F.	27 Briton St.	Asst. Cook	
Gardener, F.	Totton	Greaser	
Gatti, Luigi	Montalto, Harborough Rd.	Manager of Ritz Restaurant	313
Gear, A.	2 Stamford St., Chapel	Fireman	
Geddes, R.	80 Grove Rd.	Bedroom Steward	
GIBBONS, JACOB W.	Harbour View, Studland Bay	Saloon Steward	
Gilardino, V.	15 Bellevue Rd.	Waiter (R)	
Giles, J.	104 Lyon St.	2nd Baker	
Gill, P.	24 Waverly Rd.	Ship's Cook	
Gill, J. S.	17 Suffolk Ave.	Bedroom Steward	49
GODLEY, G.	17 Mount St.	Fireman	
Godwin, F.	Totton	Greaser	
GOLD, MRS. K.	Glenthorne, Bassett	Stewardess	
Golder, M. W.	15 Landsdowne Road	Fireman	
Gordon, J.	Sailor's Home, Southampton	Trimmer	
Goree, F.	5 Belvedere Terrace	Greaser	222
Goshawk, Arthur James	6 Coventry Rd.	3rd Saloon Steward	

NAME	ADDRESS	RATING	NUMBER
Gosling, B.	11 Lower York Street	Trimmer	
Gosling, S.	17 French St.	Trimmer	
GRAHAM, T.	28 Downpatrick St., Belfast	Fireman	
Graves, S.	8 North Front Street	Fireman	
Gregory, D.	30 Floating Bridge Rd.	Greaser	
GREGSON, MISS M.	28 Lorne Rd., Portswood	Stewardess	
Green, G.	57 Howards Grove	Trimmer	
Grodidge, E.	41 Redcliff St.	Fireman	276
Grosclaude, Gerald	8 Lumber Court, London	Asst. Coffee Man (R)	
Gunn, J. T.	23 Bridge Rd.	Asst. Steward	
Gumery, George	24 Canute Rd.	Mess Steward, Engine Dept.	
GUY, E. J.	5 College Terrace, Milton Abbas	Asst. Boots	
Gwinn, William H. Logan	Brooklyn, N.Y.	Clerk-Post Office	
HAGGAN, JOHN	Sailor's Home, Southampton	Fireman	
HAINES, ALBERT	52 Grove St.	Boatswain's Mate	
HALFORD, RICHARD	2 Latimer St.	3rd Class Steward	
Hall, F. A. J.	70 Sidney Rd.	Scullion	
Hall, J.	2 Westgate St.	Fireman	

NAME	ADDRESS	RATING	NUMBER
Hallett, G.	101 Church St.,	Fireman	
Hamblyn, E. W.	2 Norman Villas, Dyer Rd.	Bedroom Steward	
Hamilton, E.	5 Shirley Rd.	Asst. Smoke-room Steward	
Hands, B.	St. Michael's House	Fireman	
Hannan, G.	1 Oxford Terrace	Fireman	
HARDER, W.	46 Winton St.	Window Cleaner	
Harding, A.	Station Cottages, Swaythling	Asst. Pantry Steward	
HARDWICKE, REGINALD	4 Heysham Rd.	Kitchen Porter	
HARDY, JOHN	Oakleigh, Highfield	Chief 2nd Class Steward	
Harris, C. H.	14 Short St.	Bell Boy	
Harris, C. W.	14 Short St.	Saloon Steward	
Harris, E.	83 Belgrade Rd.	Fireman	
Harris, E.	13 Greenhill Ave., Winchester	Asst. Pantryman	
HARRIS, F.	57 Melville Rd., Gosport	Fireman	
Harris, F.	12 Wilton St.	Trimmer	
HARRISON, A. D.	131 Oakley Rd.	Saloon Steward	
Harrison, Norman	30 Coventry Road	Junior 2nd Engineer	
HART, JOHN EDWARD	Aberdeen, Foundry Lane	3rd Class Steward	
*Hart, Thomas	51 College St.	Fireman	

*Thomas Hart's discharge book was stolen. It was used by another who signed on in Hart's name and was lost. Hart reappeared at Southampton May 8, per his mother.

NAME	ADDRESS	RATING	NUMBER
Hartley, Wallace Henry	Surreyside West Park St., Dewsbury	Orchestra Leader	224
HARTNELL, F.	25 Argyle Rd.	Saloon Steward	
Harvey, Herbert Gifford	40 Obelisk Rd., Woolston	Jr. Asst. 2nd Engineer	
Hasgood, R.	19 Woodley Rd.	Fireman	242
Hasketh, James H.	80 Garrett Ave., Liverpool	Jr. 2nd Engineer	
Haslin, J.	Sailor's Home, Southhampton	Trimmer	
Hatch, H.	446 Portswood Road	Scullion	
Haveling, A.	South Front	Jr. Asst. 4th Engineer (Transferred 4/10/12)	
Hawkesworth, John	18 Wilton Rd.	Saloon Steward	
Hawkesworth, W.	Lemon Rd.	Asst. Dk. Steward	
Hayter, A.	10 Mayflower Road	Bedroom Steward	25
Head, A.	19 Russell St.	Fireman	
HEBB, A.	5 Bell's Court	Trimmer	
Heinen, Joseph	Norden Hill House, Lewisham	Saloon Steward	
HEMMING, SAMUEL	31 Kingsley Rd.	Lamp Trimmer	
HENDRICKSON, CHARLES	255 Northumberland Rd.	Leading Fireman	
Hendy, E.	21 Paynes Rd.	Saloon Steward	
Henry, W.	27 Romsey Rd.	Asst. Boots	

NAME	ADDRESS	RATING	NUMBER
Hensford, H. G.	132 Malmesbury Rd.	Asst. Butcher	
Hewett, T.	94 Devonfield Rd., Aintree	Bedroom Steward	168
Hill, H. P.	66 Oxford St.	Steward	
Hill, J. C.	64 Padwell Rd.	Bedroom Steward	152
Hill, J.	10 Kingsland Square	Trimmer	
Hinckley, G.	2 Oxford St.	Hospital Attendant	66
Hine, G.	Bridge St., Bruckley	3rd Baker	
Hinton, W.	26 Cumberland St.	Trimmer	85
Hiscock, S.	19 Palmerston Rd.	Plate Washer	
HITCHINS, ROBERT	43 James St., Dongola	Quartermaster	
Hoare, Leo	108 Lyon St.	Saloon Steward	
Hodge, Charles	16 Ivy Rd., Woolston	Senior Asst. 3rd Engineer	
Hodges, W.	6 Britannia Rd.	Fireman	
Hodgkinson, Leonard	67 Arthur Rd.	Senior 4th Engineer	
Hogg, Charles	24 Bulwer St., Liverpool	Bedroom Steward	
HOGG, GEORGE ALFRED	44 High St.	Look-Out-Man	
Hogue, E.	Alison Gardens, Dulwich	Plate Washer	

NAME	ADDRESS	RATING	NUMBER
Holden, Frank	Albany Rd.	Fireman (Deserted 4/10/12)	
Holland, Thomas	38 Walton Vale, Liverpool	Asst. Reception Room Steward	
Holloway, Sidney	60 Hartington Road	Asst. Clothes Presser	273
Holman, H.	Britannia Road, Northam	Able Seaman	
Hopgood, R.	81 Ramsey Rd.	Fireman	
Hopkins, F.	14 Fanshawe Street	Plate Washer	
HOPKINS, ROBERT	4 Woodstock Rd., Belfast	Able Seaman	
HORSWILL, ALBERT EDWARD JAMES	44 Derby Rd.	Able Seaman	
Hosking, George Fox	28 Avenue Rd., Itchen	Senior 3rd Engineer	
House, W.	44 Derby Rd.	Saloon Steward	
Howell, Arthur Albert	12 Cliff Rd., Itchen	Saloon Steward	319
Hughes, H.	Ivy Bank, Dyer Rd.	Asst. Chief 2nd Steward	
Humby, F.	2 Golden Grove	Plate Steward	
Hume, John Law ("Jock")	42 George St., Dumfries, Scotland	Orchestra (Violin)	193
Humphreys, H.	9 Plaswell Lane, Dolgelly	Steward	
HUMPHREYS, JAMES	113 Dukes Rd.	Quartermaster	
HUNT, A.	1 French St.	Trimmer	

NAME	ADDRESS	RATING	NUMBER
Hunt, T.	2 Queen St.	Fireman	
Hurst, C. J.	Laundry Rd.	Fireman	
HURST, WALTER	15 Chapel Rd.	Fireman	
Hutchinson, J.	91 Woodcroft Rd., Liverpool	Vegetable Cook	250
Hutchinson, J. H.	40 Onslow Rd.	Joiner & Carpenter	
HYLAND, LEO JAMES	55 Orchard Place	Steward	
Ide, T. C.	114 Lyon St.	Bedroom Steward	
Inge, W.	45 Stratton Rd.	Scullion	
Ingram, C.	18 Lower Canal Walk	Trimmer	204
Ingrouville, H.	15 Floating Bridge Rd.	Steward	
Instance, T.	12 Guillaume Terrace	Fireman	
Jackson, C.	22 Graham Rd.	Asst. Boots	
Jacobson, John	97 Dukes Rd.	Fireman	
Jago, J.	47 Millbank St.	Greaser	
Jaillet, Henry	Jamison St., London	Pastry Cook (R)	277
James, Thomas	27 College St.	Fireman	
Janaway, W. F.	Alpha House, Richmond Rd.	Bedroom Steward	
Janin, Claude	56 Seddle-scombe Rd., West Brompton, London	Soup Cook (R)	
Jarvis, W.	29 Canal Walk	Fireman	
Jeffrey, W. A.	2 Church Lane, Highfield	Controller (R)	

NAME	ADDRESS	RATING	NUMBER
Jenner, Harry	3 Bellevue Rd.	Saloon Steward	
Jensen, Charles V.	17 Morris Rd.	Saloon Steward	
JESSOP, VIOLET	71 Shirley Rd., Bedford Park, London	Stewardess	
JEWELL, ARCHIE	32 College St.	Look-Out-Man	
JOHNSON, JAMES	Sailor's Home, Southampton	Night Watch-man	
Johnston, H.	183 Albert Rd.	Asst. Ship's Cook	
Jones, A.	22 Ludlow Rd., Woolston	Plates	
Jones, Arthur E.	Carlton Rd., Woodfield	Saloon Steward	
Jones, H.	Broad St., Alresford	Roast Cook	
Jones, R. V.	7 Portland Terrace	Saloon Steward	
JONES, THOMAS	68 Nesfield St., Liverpool	Able Seaman	
Jouanwault, Georges	3 Orchard Place	Asst. Sauce Cook (R)	
JOUGHIN, CHARLES	Leighton Rd., Elmhurst	Chief Baker	
JUDD, C.	98 Derby Rd.	Fireman	
Jukes, J.	Moor Green, West End	Greaser	
Jupe, Herbert	79 Bullar Rd.	Asst. Electrician	
KASPER, F.	6 Brunswick Square	Fireman	
Kearl, C.	17 Chantry Rd.	Greaser	
Kearl, G.	31 Bay Rd., Sholing	Trimmer	

NAME	ADDRESS	RATING	NUMBER
Keegan, James	2 Cross House Rd.	Leading Fireman	
KEENE, P.	14 Rigby Rd.	Saloon Steward	
Kelland, T.	Commercial St., Bitterne	Library Steward	
Kelly, James	12 Woodleigh Road	Greaser	
Kelly, William	1 Claude Rd., Dublin	Asst. Electrician	
KEMISH, GEORGE	238 Shirley Rd.	Fireman	
Kemp, Thomas	11 Cedar Rd.	Extra Asst. 4th Engineer	
Kenchenten, Frederick	9 Latimer St.	Greaser	
Kenzler, A.	21 Blechynden Terrace	Storekeeper (Engineering Dept.)	
Kennell, C.	6 Park View	Hebrew Cook	
Kerby, W. T.	Woodminton Cottages, Salisbury	Asst. Steward	
Kerr, Thomas	7 Hanley St.	Fireman	
Ketchley, Henry	40 Northcote Road	Saloon Steward	
Kieran, M.	7 Avenue Rd.	Asst. Kitchen Storekeeper	
Kiernan, James W.	Inglewood, Bellmoor Rd.,	Chief 3rd Class Steward	
Kielford, P.	New Rd.	Steward (Left by consent 4/10/12)	
King, Alfred	132 Mile St., Gateshead-On-Tyne	Lift Attendant	238

NAME	ADDRESS	RATING	NUMBER
King, Ernest Waldron	Currin Rectory, Clones, Ireland	Clerk-Purser's Asst.	321
King, G.	46 Threefield Lane	Scullion	
King, T.	23 Middle-Market Rd., Great Yar-mouth	Master-At-Arms	
Kingscote, W. F.	24 Elgin Rd., Freemantle	Saloon Steward	
Kinsella, L.	7 Canal Walk	Fireman	
Kirkham, J.	4 Chapel St.	Greaser	
Kitching, A.	170 Derby Rd.	Saloon Steward	
Klein, H.	56 Oakley Rd.	2nd Class Barber	
KNIGHT, GEORGE	45 Ludlow Rd., Woolston	Saloon Steward	
Knight, L.	37 Spring Lane, Bishopstoke	Steward	
Knight, Robert	Employee of Harland & Wolff Belfast	Leading Hand Engineer	
KNOWLES, T.	Fanners Lane, Lymington	Fireman's Messman	
Krins, George	10 Villa Rd., Brixton, London	Orchestra (Viola)	
Lacey, Bert W.	26 Southamp-ton Rd., Salisbury	Asst. Steward	
Lahy, T.	19 Spulling Rd., East Dulwich	Fireman	
Lake, William	Florence Hotel, Southampton	Saloon Steward	

NAME	ADDRESS	RATING	NUMBER
Lane, A. E.	207 Victoria Rd., Woolston	Saloon Steward	
Latimer, A.	4 Glenwylin Row, Waterloo, Liverpool	Chief Steward	
Lauder, A.	Fenton Rd., Kelston, W. Southbourne	Asst. Confectioner	
LAVINGTON, MISS B.	Manor Farm, Headbourne Rd., Winchester	Stewardess	
Lawrence, A.	66 Oxford St.	Saloon Steward	90
LEATHER, MRS. ELIZABETH L.	28 Park Rd., Port Sunlight	Stewardess	
Lee, H.	94 Bevois St.	Trimmer	
LEE, REGINALD ROBINSON	62 Threefield Lane	Look-Out-Man	
LeFevre, George	25 Orchard Place	Saloon Steward	211
Leonard, M.	45 Charlesworth St., Belfast	Steward	
Levett, G.	5 Shirley Cottages, New Southgate	Asst. Pantryman	
LEWIS, ARTHUR	99 Radcliffe Rd.	Steward	
Light, C.	24 Lower Back of Walls	Fireman	
Light, C.	Thorney Hill, near Christ Church, Hants	Platewasher	
Light, W.	3 Marine Terrace	Fireman	

NAME	ADDRESS	RATING	NUMBER
LIGHTOLLER, CHARLES HERBERT	Nikko Lodge, Netley Abbey, Near Southampton	2nd Officer	
LINDSAY, W.	3 Coleman St.	Fireman	
LITTLEJOHN, A. J.	11 Western Terrace	Saloon Steward	
Lloyd, Humphrey	Chapel Rd., Oxford St.	Saloon Steward	
Lloyd, W.	18 Orchard Place	Fireman	
Locke, A.	309 Portswood Road	Scullion	
Long, F.	19 Sidford St.	Trimmer	
Long, W.	3 Maine Terrace	Trimmer	
Longmuir, J.	130 The Crescent, Eastleigh	Asst. Bedroom Steward	
Lovell, J.	21 Highlands Rd.	Grill Cook	
LOWE, HAROLD GODFREY	Penralet, Barmouth	5th Officer	
LUCAS, W.	3 Cardigan Terrace	Saloon Steward	
LUCAS, WILLIAM	2 Corporation Flats	Able Seaman	
Lydiatt, C.	12 Brunswick Square	Saloon Steward	
*Lyons, W. H.	27 Orchard Place	Able Seaman	
McAndrews, Thomas	Sailor's Home, Southampton	Fireman	

*Buried at sea from the Carpathia, April 16, 1912.

NAME	ADDRESS	RATING	NUMBER
McAndrews, W.	17 New Copley Rd.	Fireman	
McCarthy, F.	Charlton Rd.	Bedroom Steward	
McCARTHY, W.	9 Gratton Hill Rd., Cork, Ireland	Able Seaman	
McCastle, W.	53 French St.	Fireman	
McCawley, T. W.	22 Camden Place	Gym Instructor	
McElroy, Herbert W.	Polygon House, Southampton	Chief Purser	157
McGANN, JAMES	18 George's Place	Trimmer	
McGarvey, E.	54 College St.	Fireman	
McGaw, E.	6 Broadlands Road	Fireman	
McGOUGH, J.	St. George's St.	Able Seaman	
McGrady, James	Platform Tavern	Saloon Steward	330
McGregor, J.	7 Briton St.	Fireman	
McInerney, T.	38 Elston St., Liverpool	Greaser	
McINTYRE, WILLIAM	20 Floating Bridge Rd.	Trimmer	
McLAREN, MRS. H.	9 Shirley Rd.	Stewardess	
McMICKEN, ALFRED	43 Suffolk Ave.	Saloon Steward	
McMullen, J.	120 St. Mary's Road	Saloon Steward	
McMurray, W.	60 Empress Rd., Liverpool	Bedroom Steward	

NAME	ADDRESS	RATING	NUMBER
McQuillan, William	79 Sea View St., Belfast	Fireman	183
McRae, William	43 Threefield Lane	Fireman	
McReynolds, William M. E.	1 Lagon Villas, Belfast	Jr. 6th Asst. Engineer	
Mabey, J.	190 Albany Rd.	Steward	
MACKAY, CHARLES DONALD	18 Milton Rd.	Saloon Steward	
Mackie, George William	31 Winchester Road	Bedroom Steward	
Mackie, William Dixon	2-B Margery Park Rd., Forest Gate, London	Jr. 5th Engineer	
MAJOR, ALBERT	4 Oriental Terrace	Fireman	
Major, E.	9 Old Park Villas, Palmers Green, London	Bath Steward	
Mantle, R.	60 Brintons Rd.	Steward	
March, John S.	Newark, N.J.	Clerk (Post Office)	
Marks, J.	93 Livingstone Road	Asst. Pantryman	
Marrett, G.	32 Elm St.	Fireman	
Marriott, J. W.	7 Chilworth Rd.	Asst. Pantryman	2
MARSDEN, MISS E.	7 West Morland Terrace	Stewardess	
Marsh, F.	4 Back of Walls	Fireman	268
MARTIN, MRS. ANNIE	Fosbrooke Rd., Portsmouth	Stewardess	

NAME	ADDRESS	RATING	NUMBER
MARTIN, A.	13 High St., Fareham	Scullion	
MARTIN, MISS M. E.	1 Apsley Villa, Acton, London	2nd Cashier (R)	
Maskell, Leo	25 Albert Rd.	Trimmer	
MASON, F.	30A Waverly Road	Fireman	
Mason, J.	4 Wycombe Cottages	Leading Fireman	
Matherson, D.	20 Richmond Street	Able Seaman	192
Mathias, M.	2 Western Esplanade	Mess Steward, Deck Dept.	
Mattman, Adolf	3 Orchard Place	Iceman (R)	
MAUGE, PAUL	53 Neal St., London	Maitre D' (R)	
Maxwell, J.	27 Leighton Rd.	Carpenter	
May, A.	75 York St.	Fireman	
May, A. W.	75 York St.	Fireman's Messman	
MAYNARD, H.	21 Highlands Road	Entree Cook	
Mayo, W.	24 Cable St.	Leading Fireman	177
Maytum, A.	12 Stafford Rd.	Chief Butcher	141
MAYZES, A.	8 Commercial Street	Fireman	
Mellor, A.	6 Carlton Place	Saloon Steward	
Middleton, Alfred	Ballisodare, Sligo, Ireland	Asst. Electrician	
Middleton, M. V.	84 Felsham Rd., London	Saloon Steward	

NAME	ADDRESS	RATING	NUMBER
Milford, George	3 Graham St.	Fireman	
Millar, Robert	19 North St., Alloa, Belfast	Extra 5th Asst. Engineer	
Millar, Thomas	19 Meadow-brook St., Belfast	Asst. Deck Engineer	
MILLS, C.	94 Albert Rd.	Asst. Butcher	
Mintram, W.	15 Chapel Rd.	Fireman	
Mishellany, A.	123 Ledbury Rd., Bayswater, London	Printer	
Mitchell, B.	45 Bevois Valley	Trimmer	
Monoros, Jean	27 Tension St., London	Asst. Waiter (R)	27
Monteverdi, Giovanni	4 Queen's Park Terrace	Asst. Entree Cook (R)	
Moody, James Pell	St. James House, Grimsby	6th Officer	
Moore, A. E.	142 St. Mary's Road	Saloon Steward	
MOORE, GEORGE	51 Graham Rd.	Able Seaman	
MOORE, J. J.	64 Arthur Rd.	Fireman	
Moore, R.	Manor Cottage, Headbourne St.	Trimmer	
Moores, R.	174 Northumberland	Greaser	
Morgan, A.	18 Threefield Road	Trimmer	
Morgan, C. F.	46 Bessboro Rd., Birkenhead	Asst. Storekeeper, Kitchens	

NAME	ADDRESS	RATING	NUMBER
Morgan, Thomas	Sailor's Home, Southampton	Fireman	302
Morrell, R.	51 Malmesbury Road	Trimmer	
Morris, A.	18 Short St.	Greaser	
MORRIS, FRANK HERBERT	46 Deloune St. Fullham, London	Bath Steward	
Morris, W.	5 Marine Parade	Trimmer	
Moss, William	37 Charlton Rd.	Saloon Steward	
Moyes, William Young	11 Douglas Terrace, Stirling, Scotland	Sr. 6th Engineer	
Muller, L.	67 Oxford St.	Interpreter	
Mullin, Thomas	12 Onslow Rd.	Saloon Steward	323
Murdoch, William M.	94 Belmont Rd.	1st Officer	
MURDOCK, WILLIAM	Sailor's Home, Southampton	Fireman	
Nanineri, Francisco	34 Aubert Rd., Highbury Hill	Head Waiter (R)	
NEAL, H.	10 Cliff Rd.	Asst. Baker	
Nettleton, George	23 Empress Rd.	Fireman	
Newman, C.	9 Latimer St.	Storekeeper, Engineering	
Nichols, A.	Oak Tree Rd., St. Cloud	Boatswain	
Nicholls, T.	3 Brunswick Square	Saloon Steward	
Nichols, A. D.	43 Suffolk Ave.	Steward	
NICHOLS, W. H.	16 Kent Rd.	Steward	

NAME	ADDRESS	RATING	NUMBER
Noon, John	Sailor's Home, Southampton	Fireman	
Norris, J.	5 Spa Rd.	Fireman	
Noss, B.	8 St. Peter's Rd.	Fireman	
NOSS, HENRY	12 Black Lane	Fireman	
NUTBEAN, W.	Sportsman's Arms, High St.	Fireman	
O'CONNOR, J.	9 Tower Place	Trimmer	
O'Connor, Thomas	12 Linacre Lane, Liverpool	Bedroom Steward	
Olive, C.	43 College St.	Greaser	
Olive, Ernest R.	37 Hanley Rd.	Clothes Presser	
OLIVER, H.	15 Nichols Rd.	Fireman	
OLLIVER, ALFRED	38 Anderson Road	Quartermaster	
O'Loughlin, Dr. William Francis	Polygon House, Southampton	Chief Surgeon	
Orpet, W. H.	1 Vaudry St.	Saloon Steward	
Orr, J.	45 Coleman St.	Asst. Vegetable Cook	
Orovello, Louis	In care of Gatti	Waiter (R)	
Osborne, W.	7 Hewetts Rd., Freemantle	Saloon Steward	
OSMAN, FRANK	43 High St., Itchen	Able Seaman	
OTHEN, C.	6 Northumberland Rd.	Fireman	
Owen, L.	29 Earl's Rd.	Asst. Steward	
Pacey, R. J.	Cambridge Villa, Millbrook Rd.	Lift Attendant	

NAME	ADDRESS	RATING	NUMBER
Pacherd, Jean	3 Orchard Place	Asst. Larder (R)	
Painter, C.	172 Mortimer Road	Fireman	
Painter, Frank	10 Bridge Rd.	Fireman	
Painton, J. A.	48 Stadford St., Oxford	Captain's Steward	
Palles, T.	25 Upper Palmer St.	Greaser	
Parker, T.	Upper Boyle St.	Butcher	
Parks, Frank	Employee of Harland & Wolff, Belfast	Plumber Appren- tice	
Parr, William	Employee of Harland & & Wolff, Belfast	Asst. Manager Electrical Department	
Parsons, Edward	26 Robert's Rd.	Chief Kitchen Storekeeper	
Parsons, Frank Alfred	38 Bugle St.	Senior 5th Engineer	
Parsons, R.	Ashbrittle, near Wellington, Somerset	Saloon Steward	
PASCOE, C. H.	68 High St.	Able Seaman	
Pearce, A.	76A Holderness Rd., Bourne- mouth	Steward	
PEARCE, J.	14 Drummond Road	Fireman	
PEARCEY, ALBERT VICTOR	23 Kent Rd.	3rd Class Pantryman	
Pedrini, Alberto	Bowling Green House	Asst. Waiter (R)	

NAME	ADDRESS	RATING	NUMBER
PELHAM, G.	Sailor's Home, Southampton	Trimmer	
Penney, A.	Chantry Rd.	Trimmer (Deserted 4/10/12)	
Pennal, F.	16 West St., Shirley	Bath Steward	
Penny, W.	29 Lodge Rd.	Asst. Steward	
Penrose, John P.	30 Southview Road	Bedroom Steward	
Perkins, L.	New Inn, Soberton, Hants	Telephone Operator	
PERKINS, WALTER JOHN	Victoria Rd., Bitterne	Quartermaster	
Perotti, Alfonsi	2 Denmark Place, London	Asst. Waiter (R)	
Perrin, W.	24 Bellmoor Road	Boots	
Perracchio, Albert	4 Richmond Building, Dean St., London	Asst. Waiter (R)	
Perracchio, Sebastine	4 Richmond Building, Dean St., London	Asst. Waiter (R)	
Perriton, H.	11 St. Andrew's Road	Saloon Steward	
PERRY, E.	3 Ryde Terrace	Trimmer	
Perry, H.	3 Ryde Terrace	Trimmer	
PETERS, W. C.	114 Ludlow Rd.	Able Seaman	
Petty, Edwin Henry	26 Orchard Place	Bedroom Steward	82
Phillips, John George	Farncombe, Godalming	Sr. Marconi Operator	

NAME	ADDRESS	RATING	NUMBER
Phillips, G.	5 Grove St.	Greaser	
Phillips, J.	8 Jessie Terrace	Storeman (R)	
PHILLIMORE, H.	72 Priory Rd.	Bath Steward	
Piatti, Louis	15 Princess St., London	Asst. Waiter (R)	
Piazza, Pompeo	94 Newport Building, London	Waiter (R)	266
PIGOTT, P.	2 Windsor Terrace	Able Seaman	
Pitfield, W.	13 Albert Rd.	Greaser	
PITMAN, HERBERT JOHN	Castle Cary, Somerset	3rd Officer	
Platt, W.	107 Belgrove Road	Scullion	
PODESTA, JOHN	31 Chantry Rd.	Fireman	
Poggi, E.	Bowling Green House	Waiter (R)	301
POIGNDESTRE, JOHN	4 Elm Rd.	Able Seaman	
Poiravanti, Bertoldi	52 St. James Rd., Poultney, London	Asst. Scullery-man (R)	
Pond, G.	Sailor's Home, Southampton	Fireman	
Poök, R.	102 Alexandra Road	Asst. Bedroom Steward	
PORT, F.	Foundry Lane, Rockbourne	Steward	
PREGNALL, G.	3 Brew House Court	Greaser	

NAME	ADDRESS	RATING	NUMBER
*PRENTICE, FRANK W.	71 Denzil Ave.	Asst. Store-keeper, Kitchen	
Preston, T.	42 Millbank St.	Trimmer	
Price, Ernest	93 Grove Rd., London	Barman (R)	186
Price, R.	30 Houndwell Gardens	Fireman	
Prideaux, J. A.	23 Cotlands Rd.	Steward	
PRIEST, J.	27 Lower Canal Walk	Fireman	
PRIOR, H. J.	48 Padwell Rd.	Steward	
PRITCHARD, MRS. A.	9 Rosslyn Rd., London	Stewardess	
Proctor, C.	29 Southview Road	Chef	
Proudfoot, R.	2 Pear Tree Green	Trimmer	
Pryce, W.	Hatherdene, Newlands Rd.	Saloon Steward	
PUGH, ALFRED	72 Orchard Lane	Steward	
Pugh, Percy	22 Pell St., Northam	Leading Fireman	
PUSEY, ROBERT WILLIAM	School Lane, Hythe	Fireman	
Puzey, J. E.	61 Manor Rd., Itchen	Saloon Steward	

*At a meeting of the Titanic Historical Society in Philadelphia April 14th and 15th, 1982, Eva Hart (a passenger/survivor) told the authors that F. W. Prentice was the last surviving crew member living in England. He died in 1982.

NAME	ADDRESS	RATING	NUMBER
Randall, F. H.	182 Empress Road	Saloon Steward	
RANGER, THOMAS	81 Middle Rd.	Greaser	.
Ransom, James	72 Harrowdene Rd., Knowle, Bristol	Saloon Steward	
Ratti, Enrico	5 Lumber Court	Waiter (R)	
RAY, F. DENT	Palmer Park Ave., Bristol	Saloon Steward	
Read, J.	3 Nelson Place	Trimmer	
Reed, C.	140 Derby Rd.	Bedroom Steward	
Reed, R.	3 Wickham's Court	Trimmer	
Reeves, F.	22 Cable St.	Fireman	280
Revell, W.	102 Malmesbury Rd.	Saloon Steward	
Ricadone, Rinaldo	50 Greek St., London	Asst. Waiter (R)	
RICE, C.	12 Oriental Terrace	Fireman	
Rice, John Reginald	37 Kimberly Drive, Great Crosby, Liverpool	Asst. Purser	64
Rice, P.	40 Thackeray Road	Steward	
Richards, J.	25 Summers St.	Fireman	
Ricks, Cyril G.	1 Hanley Rd.	Asst. Storekeeper, Kitchen	100

NAME	ADDRESS	RATING	NUMBER
Rickman, G.	40 Derby Rd.	Fireman	
Ridout, W.	6 Queen Anne Buildings	Saloon Steward	
Rigozzi, Abele	6 Titchfield St., London	Waiter (R)	
Rimmer, S.	50 Cranberry Ave.	Saloon Steward	
Roberts, F.	7 Dawson Cottages	3rd Butcher	231
Roberts, G.	5 Withers Court, Reading	Fireman	
Roberts, H. H.	39 Mary Rd., Liverpool	Bedroom Steward	93
ROBERTS, MRS. M. K.	9 Chestnut Grove, Nottingham	Stewardess	
Robertson, W. G.	36 Mount St.	Asst. Steward	127
ROBINSON, MRS. ANNIE	128 Shirley Rd.	Stewardess	
Robinson, J. M.	Vine Cottage, Carlisle Rd.	Saloon Steward	151
Rogers, Edward J. W.	120 Oxford Avenue	Asst. Store-keeper, Kitchen	282
Rogers, M.	13 Greenhill Ave., Winchester	Saloon Steward	
ROSS, H.	70 Inkerman Rd., Woolston	Scullion	
Rotto, Angelo	10 West St., London	Waiter (R)	
Rous, A.	18 Ratcliffe Rd.	Plumber	
Rousseau, P.	7 Kennerton Place, London	Chef (R)	

NAME	ADDRESS	RATING	NUMBER
ROWE, GEORGE THOMAS	63 Henry St., Gosport	Quartermaster	
Rowe, M.	86 Bridge Rd.	Saloon Steward	
Rudd, H.	20 Peel St.	Storekeeper, Engine Dept.	
RULE, SAMUEL JAMES	81 Atherly Road	Bath Steward	
Rungem, T.	Middle Road	Greaser	
Russell, R.	Anchor Hotel, Redbridge	Saloon Steward	
Ryan, T.	87 Albert Rd.	Steward	
RYERSON, W. E.	18 Salop Rd, Walthamstow, London	Saloon Steward	
Saccaggi, Giovanni	22 Ponsonby Place, London	Asst. Waiter (R)	
Salussolia, Giovenez	7 Colbath Sq., London	Glassman (R)	
Samuel, O. W.	125 Osborne Road	Saloon Steward	217
Sangster, C.	83 Bevois St.	Fireman	
Sartori, Lazor	In care of Gatti	Employee (R) (Failed to join)	
Saunders, D. E.	29 Albert Rd.	Saloon Steward	
Saunders, F.	17 Sussex Terrace	Fireman	
Saunders, W.	136 Edwards Street	Fireman	
Saunders, W.	1 Southbrook Square	Trimmer	184
SAVAGE, C. J.	8 Harold Rd.	3rd Class Steward	
Sawyer, R. J.	55 Bevois St.	Window Cleaner	

NAME	ADDRESS	RATING	NUMBER
SCARROTT, JOSEPH	36 Albert Rd.	Able Seaman	
Scavino, C.	231 Hamstead Rd., London	Carver (R)	
Scott, Archibald	3 Lower Ditches	Fireman	
SCOTT, FRED	107 Clifford St.	Greaser	
Scott, J.	6 Upper Canal Walk	Asst. Boots	
Scovell, R.	141 Foundry Lane	Saloon Steward	
Sedunary, Sidney Francis	34 Emsworth Road	2nd Third Class Steward	
Self, A.	75 Romsey Rd.	Greaser	
SELF, E.	3 Kingsley Rd.	Fireman	
SENIOR, HARRY	17 South Rd., Clapham, London	Fireman	
Sesea, Gino	3 Little Poultney Chambers, Poultney, London	Waiter (R)	
Sevier, W.	Westbourne St. Mews, Paddington	Steward	
SEWARD, WILFRED	54 Stamford St., London and 5 Shirley Rd., Southampton	Chief Pantryman, 2nd Class	
Shaw, Harry	47 Towcester St., Liverpool	Scullion	
Shaw, J.	North-umberland Rd.	Fireman (Deserted 4/10/12)	

60

NAME	ADDRESS	RATING	NUMBER
Shea, John	77 Portsmouth Road	Saloon Steward	11
Shea, Thomas	18 Briton St.	Fireman	
Smillie, J.	16 Malmesbury Rd.	Saloon Steward	91
Smith, C.	35 Itchen Ferry, Hants	Scullion	
Smith, C.	Portsmouth Rd., Woolston	Bedroom Steward	329
Smith, E.	1 St. Mary's Buildings	Trimmer	
Smith, Captain Edward John	Woodhead, Winn Rd.	Commander	

(Editors note: he was fondly called "E.J." by both passengers and crew.)

NAME	ADDRESS	RATING	NUMBER
Smith, F.	33 Ordnance Road	Asst. Pantryman	
Smith, John R. Jago	England	Clerk (Post Office)	
Smith, J.	5 Sir George's Rd., Freemantle	Asst. Baker	
Smith, Jason N.	Millars Rd., Itchen	Jr. 4th Engineer	
Smith, R. G.	46 Stafford Rd.	Saloon Steward	
SMITH, MISS T. E.	Balmoral, Cobbett Rd.	Stewardess	
Smith, W.	42 Bridge Rd.	Able Seaman	
Smither, H.	1 Ash Tree Rd.	Fireman	
Snape, Mrs.	Hill Lane, Sandown	Stewardess	
Snellgrove, G.	9 Cecil Ave.	Fireman	
Snooks, W.	Sailor's Home, Southampton	Trimmer	
SNOW, E.	21 Lower Canal Walk	Trimmer	

NAME	ADDRESS	RATING	NUMBER
SPARKMAN, H.	Spring Rd., Sholing	Fireman	
Stafford, M.	4 Southbrook Square	Greaser	
Stagg, J. H.	66 Commercial Rd.	Saloon Steward	
Stanbrook, A.	36 York St.	Fireman	316
STAP, MISS S. A.	41 Bidston Ave., Birkenhead	Stewardness	
Stebbings, L.	25 Richfield Rd.	Chief Boots	
Steel, R.	No Address	Trimmer	
STEWART, JOHN	77 Earles Rd.	Steward (Veranda Cafe)	
Stocker, H.	Middle Rd., Sholing	Trimmer	
Stone, E.	91 Shirley Rd.	Bedroom Steward	243
Stone, E. J.	105 St. Andrew's Road	Bedroom Steward	41
STREET, A.	10 Crown St., Shirley	Fireman	
Stroud, A.	167 Shirley Rd.	Saloon Steward	
Stroud, E. A.	167 Shirley Rd.	Saloon Steward	
Strugnell, John	Scullers Hotel	Saloon Steward	
Stubbings, H.	North Cottage, Woodside, Lymington	Cook & Steward's Mess	
Stubbs, H.	11 Spa Road	Fireman	
SHEATH, FREDERICK	12 Bell St.	Trimmer	
Shepherd, Jonathan	16 Bellevue Terrace	Jr. Asst. 2nd Engineer	
Shillaber, Charles	21 Nelson Rd.	Trimmer	195

NAME	ADDRESS	RATING	NUMBER
SHIRES, ALFRED	5 Peel St.	Fireman	
*Siebert, S. C.	8 Harold Rd., Shirley	Bedroom Steward	
Simmonds, F. C.	203 Middle-brook Rd.	Saloon Steward	
SIMMONS, A.	80 Bevois Valley Road	Scullion	
Simmons, W.	2 Thackeray Road	Passenger Cook	
Simpson, Dr. J. Edward	Packenham Rd., Belfast	Asst. Surgeon	
Sims, W.	Charlotte St.	Fireman (Left by consent 4/10/12)	
Skeats, W.	29 King St.	Trimmer	
Skinner, E.	Criterion Restaurant, Oxford St.	Saloon Steward	
Slade, A.	Chantry Rd.	Fireman (Deserted 4/10/12)	
Slade, D.	Chantry Rd.	Fireman (Deserted 4/10/12)	
Slade, Thomas	Chantry Rd.	Fireman (Deserted 4/10/12)	
Slight, H. J.	48 Bellevue St.	Steward	
Slight, W.	Hillside, Broadland Rd.	Larder Cook	
SLOAN, MISS MARY	1 Kersland Rd., Belfast	Stewardess	
Sloan, Peter	77A Clovelly Road	Chief Electrician	

*Buried at sea from the Carpathia, April 15, 1912.

NAME	ADDRESS	RATING	NUMBER
SLOCOMBE, MAUDE	8 Leopold Terrace, Tottenham, London	Masseuse (Turkish Bath)	
Small, W.	14 Russell St., Liverpool	Leading Fireman	
Sullivan, S.	27 Marsh Lane	Fireman	
Swan, W.	62 Hale Rd., Walton, Liverpool	Bedroom Steward	
Symonds, J.	61 Church St.	Saloon Steward	
SYMONS, GEORGE	55 Franchise St., Weymouth	Look-Out-Man	
Talbot, G. F. C.	4 Alpha Villas, Lemon Rd., Shirley	Steward	150
Tamlyn, Frederick	20 Southampton St.	Mess Steward, Deck Dept.	123
Taylor, C.	85 High St.	Able Seaman	
Taylor, C.	5 Oxford St.	Steward	
Taylor, F.	94 Manor Rd.	Fireman	
Taylor, J.	23 Queen's St.	Fireman	
TAYLOR, JAMES	35 Russell St.	Fireman	
Taylor, Leonard	6 Sherbourne Rd., Blackpool	Turkish Bath Attendant	
Taylor, Percy C.	9 Fentiman Rd., Clapham, London	Orchestra (Cellist)	
Taylor, W.	43 Morris Rd.	Saloon Steward	
TAYLOR, W. H.	2 Broad St.	Fireman	
Terrell, B.	2 Trinity Cottages	Able Seaman	

NAME	ADDRESS	RATING	NUMBER
TERRELL, F.	5 Grove St.	Asst. Steward	
Testoni, Ercole	32-A St. James Buildings, Little Poulteney St., London	Asst. Glass-man (R)	
Thaler, M.	19 Station Rd., W. Croydon	Steward	
THESSINGER, A.	102 French St.	Bedroom Steward	
THOMAS, A. C.	11 Brunswick Road	Saloon Steward	
THOMAS, B.	122 Avenue Rd.	Saloon Steward	
Thomas, James	20 Newman St.	Fireman	
Thompson, H.	Eastwood, Lumsden Ave.	2nd Storekeeper, Kitchen	
THOMPSON, JOHN	Primrose Hill, 2 House, Liverpool	Fireman	
Thorley, William	18 John St.	Asst. Cook	
THRELFALL, T.	128 St. Martin's Court	Leading Fireman	
THRESHER, G.	36 Mount Pleasant Rd.	Fireman	
Tietz, Carlo	Richmond Tavern, Bridgewood	Kitchen Porter (R)	
Tizard, A.	23 Lower York Street	Fireman	
TOMS, F.	Bitterne Park	Saloon Steward	
Topp, T.	89 Millbrook Rd., Farn-borough	2nd Butcher	
Tozer, J.	6 Chattis St.	Greaser	

NAME	ADDRESS	RATING	NUMBER
TRIGGS, R.	3 Canal Walk	Fireman	
Tucker, B.	43 Suffolk Ave.	2nd Pantry-man	
Turley, R.	Sailor's Home, Southampton	Fireman	
Turner, G. F.	Bond Rd., Anberry	Stenographer	
Turner, L.	19 Terminus Terrace	Saloon Steward	23
Turvey, Charles	90 Cornwall Rd., London	Page Boy (R)	
Urbini, Robert	16 Manette St., London	Waiter (R)	
Valassori, Ettera	7 Great Russell St., London	Waiter (R)	
Veal, A.	15 Imperial Avenue	Greaser	
Veal, T.	20 Forster Mount	Saloon Steward	
Vear, H.	2 Spa Gardens	Fireman	
Vear, W.	2 Spa Gardens	Fireman	59
Vicat, Jean	13 Howley St., London	Fish Cook (R)	
Villablange, Pierre	8 Rue National, Albroise, France	Asst. Soup Cook (R)	
Vine, H.	55 Leith Mansions, London	Asst. Controller (R)	
Vioni, R.	8 Lynton Man-sions, London	Waiter (R)	
Vogelin, H.	8 Lumber Court, London	Coffeeman (R)	

NAME	ADDRESS	RATING	NUMBER
Wake, L.	2 Glouster Passage	Asst. Baker	
Wallis, Mrs.	23 St. Mary's Street	Matron, 3rd Class	
Walpole, J.	12 Stafford Rd.	Chief Pantryman	
Walsh, Miss Katherine	57 Church Rd.	Stewardess	
Ward, Arthur	Manor House, Romsey	Jr. Asst. 4th Engineer	
Ward, E.	6 Blechynden Terrace	Bedroom Steward	
Ward, J.	22 James St.	Leading Fireman	
Ward, P.	36 Richmond Terrace, Shirley	Bedroom Steward	
WARD, WILLIAM	107 Millbrook Road	Saloon Steward	
Wardner, F.	45 Endle St.	Fireman	
Wareham, Robert Arthur	46 Park Rd.	Bedroom Steward	246
Warwick, T.	Totton, Hants	Saloon Steward	
Wateridge, E.	Millbrook Rd.	Fireman	
Watson, Ennis Hastings	Employee of Harland & Wolff Belfast	Electrical Apprentice	
Watson, W. A.	23 Oakley Rd.	Bell Boy	
Watson, W.	13 York St.	Fireman	158
Weatherstone, Tom	5 Kenilworth Road	Saloon Steward	
Webb, Brooke	34 Hanley Rd.	Smoke Room Steward	

NAME	ADDRESS	RATING	NUMBER
Webb, S.	Sailor's Home, Southampton	Trimmer	
Webber, F.	49 Avenue Rd.	Leading Fireman	
WEIKMAN, AUGUST H.	9 Dyer Rd., Ivybank	Barber	
Welch, H.	Bond Rd., Bitterne Park	Asst. Cook	
WELLER, WILLIAM	Holyrood House	Able Seaman	
WHEAT, JOSEPH THOMAS	14 Cobden Gardens, Bitterne	Asst. 2nd Steward	
WHEELTON, EDWARD	Norwood House, Shirley	Saloon Steward	
White, Arthur	36 Purbrook Rd., Portsmouth	Asst. Barber	247
WHITE, ALFRED	3 Southampton Place	Greaser	
White, F.	14 Northbrook Road	Trimmer	
White, J.	41 Thackeray Rd.	G. H. Steward	272
White, L.	248 Romsey Rd.	Saloon Steward	
WHITE, WILLIAM GEORGE	9 Coblens St., Woking	Trimmer	
WHITELEY, THOMAS	29 St. John's Park, Highgate, London	1st Class Saloon Steward	
Whitford, A.	33 Richmond Street	Saloon Steward	
WIDGERY, JAMES G.	25 Rokeby Ave. Bristol	2nd Class Bath Steward	

68

NAME	ADDRESS	RATING	NUMBER
Wilde, Henry T.	25 Grey Rd., Walton, Liverpool	Chief Officer	
Willis, W.	59 Derby Rd.	Steward	
Williams, Arthur J.	52 Peter Rd., Walton, Liverpool	Asst. Store-keeper, Kitchen	
Williams, E.	2 Canal Walk	Fireman	
WILLIAMS, W.	52 Northum-berland Rd.	Asst. Steward	
Williamson, James B.	England	Clerk (Post Office)	
Wilson, Bertie	40 Richmond Rd., Shirley	Senior 2nd Asst. Engineer	
Wilton, William	5 Queen's St.	Trimmer	
Wiltshire, W.	8 Britannia Rd.	Asst. Butcher	
WINDEBANK, A.	Elmhurst, Shirley	Sauce Cook	
Witcher, A.	9 Wilson Place	Fireman	
Witt, F.	St. Michael's House	Trimmer	
Witt, H.	28 Lower Cottage St.	Fireman	
WITTER, JAMES	56 Porchester Rd., Woolston	Smoke Room Steward	
Wittman, H.	12 Richville Rd.	Bedroom Steward	315
Wood, J. T.	7 Norfolk Rd., Upper Clapton, London	Asst. Steward	
Woods, H.	St. Michael's House	Trimmer	
Woodford, F.	14 Clovelly Rd.	Greaser	163

NAME	ADDRESS	RATING	NUMBER
Woodward, Jack W.	The Firs, Windmill Rd., Headington, Oxfordshire	Orchestra (Pianist)	
Woody, Oscar S.	Washington, D. C.	Clerk (Post Office)	167
Wormald, F.	5 Testwood Rd.	Saloon Steward	144
Wrapson, H.	33 Southampton St.	Asst. Pantryman	
Wright, Fred	12 Steur St., Shepherd's Bush, London	Squash Court Attendant	
Wright, William	9 Emsworth Rd.	G. H. Steward	
Wyeth, J.	14 Millbank St.	Fireman	
WYNN, WALTER	8 Church St.	Quartermaster	
YEARSLEY, H.	6 Glouster Passage	Saloon Steward	
Yoshack, J.	103 Malmesbury Rd.	Saloon Steward	
Young, F.	28 Russell St.	Fireman	
Zanetti, Mario	Cairo Cafe, 3 Soho St., London	Asst. Waiter (R)	
Zarracchi, L.	9 Orchard Place	Wine Butler (R)	

COAL, STEAM AND GUTS

by Patrick D. Peters

BELL, BAINES, ABRAMS, BELLOWS, COX, BANNON, BEVIS... "Men, you have done your full duty, you can do no more." KEARL, BURROWS, WOODFORD, LEE, BRUTON, VEAL, LONG . . . With these words at 2:05 A.M. on the morning of April 15, 1912, Captain E. J. Smith dismissed from their duties Marconi operators Phillips and Bride. Indeed, in those early morning hours outstanding acts of heroism and selflessness had been performed by crew members and passengers alike, but below decks, far from the sights and sounds of boats being lowered into the water, there labored over 340 crewmen. These were the men of *Titanic's* engine department.

BUTT, LONG, MCANDREWS, CHERRETT, MCANDREWS, CHORLEY... Just working below the waterline in an Atlantic mail steamer was an act of bravery in itself. Life on these ships was hot, dirty, physically demanding and often dangerous in just normal day-to-day operations.

MCCASTLE, COPPERTHWAITE, CORCORAN, MITCHELL, COTTON, MOORE... The men who serviced the 29 huge boilers and 3 engines were divided into 6 main classifications: engineers, electricians, boilermakers, greasers, trimmers and firemen.

CROSS, MORGAN, CUNNINGHAM, MORRELL, CURTIS, MORRIS, DAVIES... Aboard that night were 196 firemen and 77 trimmers. They worked in four-hour shifts, two shifts per day. Their work was supervised by 13 leading firemen, one assigned to each boiler room and working a twelve-hour shift.

PERRY, PRESTON, DOYLE, PROUDFOOT, FORD, READ, FRASER . . . The fireman's job was tending the fires in the furnaces. He would shovel coal in as needed to keep "steam up" and would work the fires with "slices," that is, use long-handled tools to break up slag build-up and keep the bed of hot coals smooth and even.

REED, GEAR, PENNEY, GOLDER, SAUNDERS, SCOTT, GRAVES . . . The trimmers moved the coal from the bunkers to a location close at hand to the men stoking the fires. The name "trimmer" came from the fact that these men kept the ship in "trim" or "even" by removing equal amounts of coal from both port and starboard bunkers.

SHILLABER, GRODIDGE, SKEATS, HALL, SMITH, HALLETT, SNOOKS . . . In the course of one single watch, these men would move, by wheelbarrow and shovel, over 20,000 pounds of coal. All this was done in an environment with temperatures in excess of 101 degrees, in the dead of winter, and high humidity caused by the many minor leaks so common to any steam producing operation.

STEEL, HANDS, STOCKER, HANNAN, HARRIS . . . These men were also constantly surrounded by coal dust which covered everything like "black snow." It got on—or in—you, and it was highly explosive. Some worked on ships where boiler safeties were "tied down" in order to gain a knot or two more speed. The end result being, more often than not, a devastating explosion of the same boiler.

WEBB, HART, WHITE, HASGOOD, WILTON, HEAD, WITT . . . It is easy to see why so many of the men who worked in the stokeholds of "Mail Steamers" and other ships would become physically strong and brutal. This, however, was not the case on "Titanic." The men were physically tough and capable, but they were still human. There was a sense of compassion universal to these men. The fact that a freezing member of this group refused a warm coat in one of the life boats so it could be given to a cold young girl is proof of this.

WOODS, HODGES, HOLDEN, HOPGOOD, HUNT, HURST . . . They had a strong, but gruff, camaraderie among them—not unlike that of soldiers in wartime. The loyalty to their "mates" was so strong, in fact, that one man, who had been drawing the fires in Boiler Room #4 and left when the water reached his thighs, returned because he felt he had run out on his friends. They were the same as their fellow crew members above deck—superstitious, had a sense of humor, respected women and loved their families.

JACOBSON, JAMES, JARVIS, KEEGAN, KERR, KINSELLA, LAHY . . . Things were actually quite easy that Monday morning. The ship, being new, did not require much effort to maintain steam pressure. So most of the firemen and trimmers were working their boilers in t-shirts and more or less relaxing. Some brewed tea and one or two were fixing snacks on the machinery, which was often used as makeshift stoves.

LIGHT, C., LIGHT, W., LLOYD, MCGARVEY, MCGAW, MCGREGOR, MCRAE . . . To the men in Boiler Room #6 goes the "honor" of being the first people aboard to know that the 'berg had indeed holed the ship. As the sea poured in, these men started a back-breaking race with the sea. They had to get the dampers shut and the fires drawn and put out to prevent the icy Atlantic brine from causing an explosion as it reached the hot boilers. This activity would go on all over the ship several more times before the morning was over. Some men, like John Thompson, would be burned doing their job, but it had to be done. Everyone knew what horrible things would happen to struggling passengers in the water if the Atlantic suddenly began to boil from water hitting lit boilers.

MCQUILLAN, MARRETT, MARSH, MASON, MAY, MAYO . . . The boiler room men did a superb job that night. But because of their devotion to duty, only 63 of the 275 firemen, trimmers and boiler makers survived that ordeal.

MILFORD, MINTRAM, MORGAN, NETTLETON, NOON, NORRIS . . . *"Titanic"* also carried a compliment of 34 greasers and 26 engineers. The exact number of engineers is debatable, however, since no two references refer to the same number, the above quoted total comes from the first edition of The Titanic Historical Society's *Crew List* and uses only those names listed with "engineer" beside them.

PAINTER, C., PAINTER, F., POND, PRICE, PUGH, REEVES . . . Under the leadership of Chief Engineer Bell, these 60 men had the responsibility for operating and maintaining all the steam powered machinery aboard that mammoth ship.

RICHARDS, RICKMAN, ROBERTS, SANGSTER, SAUNDERS, F., SAUNDERS, W. . . . These men worked in the boiler rooms on all of the draft fans which aided the efficient burning of the coal. They were in charge of the evaporators which distilled sea water into fresh water to feed the pressure vessels that the fires heated. They adjusted the throttles to match the speed requested by the bridge. A constant watch had to be kept on the condensor vacuum and the feedwater pump pressures. Steam chest pressures had to be maintained as did the packings on the shafts of the two huge four-cylinder reciprocating engines. There was also the central turbine to maintain, eight large dynamos and other auxiliary machinery, as well as cleanliness of the compartments. All of this was done in a hot, steamy atmosphere with an almost-unbelievable noise level.

SHAW, SHEA, SIMS, SLADE, A., SLADE, D., SLADE, T., SMALL . . . Shortly after the alarms sounded and the huge-geared, watertight doors closed notch-by-notch, all of their priorities changed. Their attention shifted from the main engines that were rated at 50,000 horse power and could make up to 24 knots, to keeping steam supplied to the dynamos and keeping the boiler rooms dry at least until the fires were out.

ADAMS, ALSOPP, DODD, BEATTIE, CHISWALL, BREWER, ALLEN . . . There is no evidence that day that these men consciously thought of leaving. They seemed consumed with their duties and went about doing whatever had to be done to conserve power. Forty-five of the electric fans in the engine room were shut down, as were any unnecessary fans in the boiler rooms.

DODDS, BOTT, ERVINE, FITZPATRICK, BROOKS, BAILEY, DYER . . . Through their efforts, several of the boiler rooms were kept fairly free of the ever encroaching sea water. Even Boiler Room #5 with its two-foot-long gash was kept dry enough for the firemen to put out the fires. Engineers Harvey and Shepherd were occupied in doing this for quite a while. Steam from lifting safeties and smoke from the fires made vision very limited. One deck plate had been removed for better access to the pump lines. Shepherd fell into this opening and broke his leg. He was moved into the pump room for relative comfort.

CASTLEMAN, JUPE, CALDERWOOD, BALL, FARQUHARSON, COUCH, KELLY . . . Not long after this, the bulkhead between #6 and #5 boiler rooms gave way. Engineer Harvey yelled to the others to get out. He himself headed for the pump room to get his comrade. The last person to see him stated he saw him go under the swirling waters. It is highly possible that these two men down so far below the decks were the first of the many fatalities that night.The best epitaph for Engineer Harvey should be, "No greater love hath a man than to lay down his life for his friends."

CARR, BARLOW, FRASER, MIDDLETON, BARNES . . . Around 2 A.M., the engineers, having been relieved of their duties, trooped up to the boat deck. They all, at this time, must have had some pretty profound and sorrowful thoughts about home and loved ones they knew they would never see again. One in particular must have felt especially unfortunate. He was Jr. 2nd Engineer Hasketh. His billet was supposed to have gone to a Colin MacDonald, but MacDonald had a bad feeling about this maiden voyage and refused the sizable promotion three times and did not go. So the 2nd Engineer's good fortune had now gone sour.

HARVEY, FAY, COE, BENDELL, HASKETH, GARDENER, COOPER, BENNETT, HAVELING . . . One can only imagine how they spent those last few minutes on a boat deck devoid of boats and with no life jackets to wear. The lack of life jackets could account for there being only four survivors of these 60 men and only one body ever being recovered.

GODWIN, CRABB, BENVILLE, HODGE, GO-REE, DAWSON, BESSANT . . . From just after the collision until the end, all of these men had just three main duties. They had to get the boilers secured, keep pumps running as long as possible and finally keep steam going to the ship's generators for as long as they could.

HODGKINSON, GREGORY, EAGLE, BIDDLESCOMB, HOSKING, JAGO, ELLIOTT . . . There were six men who were responsible for maintaining the flow of electricity aboard this ship. The eight generators in their care were capable of supplying power to a small city which indeed the *Titanic* was. This power was used in everything from the electric cranes on the promenade and saloon decks to the lamps in every passageway and cabin. This ship had all the latest electric-powered amenities.

BIGGS, KEMP, JUKES, EVANS, BLACK, MCREYNOLDS, KEARL... Electrified ships weren't a new thing. Indeed, electricity on ships had existed since the 1880's and being a marine electrician was one of the few "technical specialties" in the merchant service at that time.

FERRARY, BLACK, MACKIE, KELLY, FORD, BLACKMAN ... On April 15th, the electricians had three primary work stations. They all worked in the electric engine room aft of the turbine engine room at first, as well as in the switchboard room located on the orlop deck. Here they shifted the load from the various circuits to keep the ship well lit and only necessary powered equipment operating. They consulted with Chief Engineer Bell and had unneeded fans and other auxiliary equipment shut down to save the badly needed power.

KENCHENTEN, DICKSON, BLAKE, BARRETT, MILLAR ... But during the hustle and bustle of that fateful night, there is evidence that their composure, like that of most of the engine department, remained calm. In fact, it is reported that greaser Alfred White actually brewed himself a cup of coffee while at his post near the dynamos.

KIRKHAM, GORDON, BLANEY, PARSONS, MCINERNEY, GOSLING, BLANN ... The situation became more and more untenable during the last half hour and eventually their duties shifted to the last of their areas—the emergency dynamo room located on the saloon deck. It was behind the second class pantry and within the base of the #4 funnel. From here, power was kept up and the lights on until 2:18 A.M. at which time all the lights glowed a "devilish red" and went out forever. At this time, these six men took leave of their posts and headed up to the open decks. We can only imagine what they went through. They had to climb up stairs that by this time were tilted at almost an impossible angle and had to do this in pitch darkness. They had only two minutes to make it—the ship foundered at 2:20 A.M. Most likely they were drowned after the ship sank. It must have been hell to be trapped below decks, in darkness, with foamy sea water cascading down upon them and nowhere to run.

SHEPHERD, MOORES, GOSLING, SMITH, MORRIS, GREEN . . . Of these six men, none survived and not one body was ever recovered.

BRADLEY, WARD, OLIVE, HARRIS, WILSON, PALLES... The sacrifices and devotion to duty of all the members of the engine department accomplished two things. First, it gave the men on deck sufficient light to see what they were doing and allowed them to safely lower the boats and save passengers. Secondly, it gave Phillips and Bride power enough to send distress messages up to 2:05 A.M. and aid resuce ships by giving information and directions.

HASLIN, BROWN, CREESE, PHILLIPS, HILL, BROWN, MILLAR . . . But, bravery is often a two-edged sword. In one case, lives are saved and on the other hand, lives are lost.

RUNGEM, HINTON, SELF, INGRAM, BURROUGHS, STAFFORD . . . Let us consider the obverse side of their unselfish acts. It was noted by Mr. Beesley that even the "wounded *Titanic* gave every one a feeling of security." It is, in fact, reported that John Jacob Astor noted that "we are safer here than in that little boat." Consider that these feeling of comfort, safety and security were not caused so much by the *Titanic's* size as by the fact that she was well-lighted while the lifeboats were not and she was still warmed, unlike the boats. What would have happened if the heat and lights had failed earlier on, let's say 12:30 or 1:00 A.M.? Would perhaps 100 or 200 more people have gotten into the boats? It is just possible that the total saved could have risen had the vessel been less hospitable than it seemed to be. Of course, hindsight is always the clearest form of vision, but ask "What if?"

SMITHER, SNELLGROVE, STANBROOK, STUBBS, SULLIVAN, TAYLOR, J., TAYLOR, F. . . . The average pay of these men was five pounds a month and those who survived lost this and all of their worldly possessions as the ship disappeared beneath the waves. The rest paid the supreme price for their bravery and adherence to their duty. They are not forgotten, however, for from that time up to this very day, the official British Merchant navy's color for its marine engineers has been royal purple, in their honor.

THOMAS, THOMPSON, TIZARD, TURLEY, VEAR, H. . . . Among these men are represented fathers, sons, and brothers. They came from Southampton, Belfast, St. Denny's, Totton, Woolston, Dublin, London, Stirling, Itchen, Romsey, Eastleigh, Northam, Liverpool, Chapel, Sholing, Dulwich, Freemantle, Hants, and Northampton—they were missed by all.

VEAR, W., WARD, WARDNER, WATERIDGE, WATSON, WEBBER . . . Some of the most splendid acts of individual bravery exhibited that night will never really be known except to those who performed them and to their God. There were no living witnesses. Most assuredly though, the final entry in their "Book of Life" by the commander of All Lives had to have been a "well done." They richly

deserved it. WILLIAMS, WITCHER, WITT, WYETH,
YOUNG . . .

Patrick D. Peters
Vineland, New Jersey
Life Member, Titanic Historical Society

Pictured here are the three Halifax,
of the *Titanic*

Photo courtesy Charles Haas
This sign in Fairview Cemetery gives one solemn thoughts.

Photo courtesy Elizabeth L. Watson
Fairview Cemetery, four rows of *Titanic* dead.

Nova Scotia cemeteries where some *dead lie buried.*

Photo courtesy Russ Lownds
Baron von Hirsch Hebrew Cemetery.

Photo courtesy Elizabeth Watson
Mt. Olivet Roman Catholic Cemetery.

Photo courtesy Charles Haas
The Public Archives of Nova Scotia, Halifax.

Photo courtesy Elizabeth L. Watson
The entrance to the Fairview Cemetery.

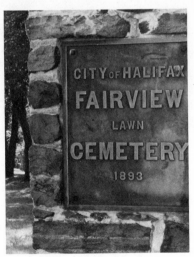

Photo courtesy Charles Haas

Mt. Olivet Roman Catholic Cemetery. 14 identified bodies buried and 5 unidentified.

The marker of Ernest King, *Titanic* clerk, Purser's Assistant. Courtesy of Russ Lownds, Halifax, N.S.

The marker of John Hume, violinist.

Photos courtesy Charles Haas
The marker of J. Fred Clarke, bass player in the *Titanic's* band.

Photo courtesy Elizabeth L. Watson
The marker of J. Brown, Fireman

Photo courtesy Charles Haas
A view showing the rows of *Titanic* graves in Fairview Cemetery.

The marker of Ernest Edward
Samuel Freeman on crew list as
Chief Deck Steward.

The marker for George H. Dean, Assistant Steward.

Photo courtesy Russ Lownds
Everett Edward was a trimmer on board the *Titanic*.

Photo courtesy Elizabeth L. Watson
The marker for James McGrady, Saloon Steward.

DISPOSITION OF IDENTIFIED CREW MEMBERS

NO.	NAME	INTERRED	DATE
2	Marriott, J. W.	In Fairview Cemetery, Row 4	May 8, 1912
10	Butt, R.	In Fairview Cemetery Row 4	May 8, 1912
11	Shea, John	In Fairview Cemetery, Row 3	May 7, 1912
23	Turner, L.	At Sea from Mackay-Bennett	April 21, 1912
25	Hayter, A.	At Sea from Mackay-Bennett	April 21, 1912
27	Monoros, Jean	At Sea from Mackay-Bennett	April 21, 1912
34	Ashe, H. W.	In Fairview Cemetery, Row 4	May 8, 1912
41	Stone, E. F.	At Sea from Mackay-Bennett	April 21, 1912
49	Gill, S.	At Sea from Mackay-Bennett	April 21, 1912
59	Vear, W.	At Sea from Mackay-Bennett	April 22, 1912
64	Rice, John Reginald	In Fairview Cemetery, Row 4	May 8, 1912
66	* Hinckley, G.	At Sea from Mackay-Bennett	April 22, 1912
77	Butt, W.	At Sea from Mackay-Bennett	April 24, 1912
82	Petty, Edwin H.	At Sea from Mackay-Bennett	April 24, 1912
83	Dashwood, Will G.	In Fairview Cemetery, Row 4	May 6, 1912
85	Hinton, W.	At Sea from Mackay-Bennett	April 24, 1912

NO.	NAME	INTERRED	DATE
90	Lawrence, A.	*Body claimed by his widow	
91	Smillie, J.	At Sea from Mackay-Bennett	April 23, 1912
93	Roberts, H. H.	At Sea from Mackay-Bennett	April 23, 1912
100	Ricks, Cyril G.	At Sea from Mackay-Bennett	April 24, 1912
107	Boothby, W.	At Sea from Mackay-Bennett	April 24, 1912
111	Chiswall, George Alexander	At Sea from Mackay-Bennett	April 23, 1912
116	Butterworth, J.	At Sea from Mackay-Bennett	April 24, 1912
123	Tamlyn, Frederick	At Sea from Mackay-Bennett	April 24, 1912
127	Robertson, W. G.	At Sea from Mackay-Bennett	April 23, 1912
138	Fellowes, A.	In Fairview Cemetery, Row 3	May 6, 1912
141	Maytum, A.	In Fairview Cemetery, Row 1	May 8, 1912
144	Wormald, F.	In Hebrew Cemetery	May 3, 1912
145	Allen, Henry	In Fairview Cemetery, Row 4	May 8, 1912
146	Anderson, Walter J.	At Sea from Mackay-Bennett	April 24, 1912
150	Talbot, G.F.C.	In Fairview Cemetery, Row 4	May 8, 1912
151	Robinson, J. M.	At Sea from Mackay-Bennett	April 24, 1912

*Shipped to Rockford, Essex, England

NO.	NAME	INTERRED	DATE
152	Hill, J. C.	At Sea from Mackay-Bennett	April 24, 1912
157	McElroy, Herbert	At Sea from Mackay-Bennett	April 24, 1912
158	Watson, W.	At Sea from Mackay-Bennett	April 24, 1912
159	Barker, Ernest T.	At Sea from Mackay-Bennett	April 24, 1912
161	Bailey, G.F.	In Fairview Cemetery, Row 3	May 8, 1912
163	Woodford, F.	In Fairview Cemetery, Row 3	May 6, 1912
167	Woody, Oscar S.	At Sea from Mackay-Bennett	April 24, 1912
168	Hewett, T.	At Sea from Mackay-Bennett	April 24, 1912
177	Mayo, W.	At Sea from Mackay-Bennett	April 24, 1912
183	McQuillan, Wm.	In Fairview Cemetery, Row 3	May 6, 1912
184	Saunders, W.	At Sea from Mackay-Bennett	April 24, 1912
186	Price, Ernest	In Fairview Cemetery, Row 4	May 8, 1912
192	Matherson, D.	In Fairview Cemetery, Row 4	May 8, 1912
193	Hume, John Law	In Fairview Cemetery, Row 1	May 8, 1912
195	Shillaber, Charles	In Fairview Cemetery, Row 4	May 8, 1912
200	Davies, J. J.	At Sea from Mackay-Bennett	April 24, 1912
202	Clarke, J. Fred	In Mt. Olivet Cemetery	May 8, 1912

NO.	NAME	INTERRED	DATE
204	Ingram, C.	In Fairview Cemetery, Row 3	May 6, 1912
205	Akerman, J.	In Fairview Cemetery, Row 3	May 6, 1912
211	LeFevre, George	In Fairview Cemetery, Row 3	May 6, 1912
212	Delandes, Percy	In Fairview Cemetery, Row 1	May 6, 1912
215	Bernardi, Baptiste	In Mt. Olivet Cemetery	May 8, 1912
217	Samuel, O. W.	In Fairview Cemetery, Row 1	May 8, 1912
218	Cave, Herbert	In Fairview Cemetery, Row 4	May 8, 1912
221	Allaria, Baptiste	In Fairview Cemetery, Row 3	May 6, 1912
222	Goree, F.	In Fairview Cemetery, Row 3	May 6, 1912
224	Hartley, Wallace H.	*Colne, Lancashire, England	May 18, 1912
227	Dawson, J.	In Fairview Cemetery, Row 3	May 8, 1912
231	Roberts, F.	In Fairview Cemetery, Row 4	May 8, 1912
235	Baxter, Thomas	In Fairview Cemetery, Row 3	May 6, 1912
238	King, Alfred	In Fairview Cemetery, Row 4	May 8, 1912
239	Freeman, Ernest	In Fairview Cemetery, Row 4	May 10, 1912
242	Hasgood, R.	In Fairview Cemetery, Row 3	May 6, 1912

*Body claimed by his father, A. Hartley, and shipped to England via Boston on the *Arabic* 5/7/12.

NO.	NAME	INTERRED	DATE
243	Stone, E. J.	In Fairview Cemetery, Row 1	May 6, 1912
244	Debreuca, Maurice	In Mt. Olivet Cemetery	May 8, 1912
246	Wareham, Robert Arthur	In Fairview Cemetery, Row 3	May 6, 1912
247	White, Arthur	In Fairview Cemetery, Row 4	May 8, 1912
250	Hutchinson, J.	In Fairview Cemetery, Row 4	May 10, 1912
251	Carney, William	In Fairview Cemetery, Row 3	May 6, 1912
252	Dean, George H.	In Fairview Cemetery, Row 3	May 6, 1912
266	Piazza, Pompeo	In Mt. Olivet Cemetery	May 10, 1912
267	Brown, J.	In Fairview Cemetery, Row 3	May 6, 1912
268	Marsh, F.	In Fairview Cemetery, Row 4	May 8, 1912
270	Deeble, Alfred	In Fairview Cemetery, Row 1	May 3, 1912
272	White, J.	In Fairview Cemetery, Row 4	May 8, 1912
273	Holloway, Sidney	In Fairview Cemetery, Row 3	May 6, 1912
274	Bogie, L.	In Fairview Cemetery, Row 1	May 8, 1912
276	Grodidge, E.	In Fairview Cemetery, Row 3	May 6, 1912
277	Jaillet, Henry	In Mt. Olivet Cemetery	May 10, 1912
280	Reeves, F.	In Fairview Cemetery, Row 4	May 7, 1912

NO.	NAME	INTERRED	DATE
282	Rogers, Edward J. W.	In Fairview Cemetery, Row 4	May 8, 1912
290	Bristow, R. C.	In Fairview Cemetery, Row 3	May 6, 1912
300	Cox, Will Denton	In Fairview Cemetery, Row 3	May 7, 1912
301	Poggi, E.	In Fairview Cemetery, Row 4	May 8, 1912
302	Morgan, Thomas	In Mt. Olivet Cemetery	May 8, 1912
311	Donati, Italo	In Fairview Cemetery, Row 4	May 10, 1912
313	Gatti, Luigi	In Fairview Cemetery, Row 4	May 10, 1912
315	Wittman, H.	In Fairview Cemetery, Row 4	May 10, 1912
316	Stanbrook, A.	In Fairview Cemetery, Row 4	May 10, 1912
317	Elliott, Edward	In Fairview Cemetery, Row 4	May 10, 1912
319	Howell, Arthur Albert	In Fairview Cemetery, Row 4	May 10, 1912
320	Cartwright, James Edward	In Fairview Cemetery, Row 4	May 10, 1912
321	King, Ernest Waldron	In Fairview Cemetery, Row 4	May 10, 1912
323	Mullin, Thomas	In Fairview Cemetery, Row 4	May 10, 1912
329	Smith, C.	In Fairview Cemetery, Row 1	May 20, 1912
330*	McGrady, James	In Fairview Cemetery, Row 2	June 12, 1912

*The body of James McGrady was picked up by the S.S. ALGERINE and taken to St. John's, Newfoundland. From there it was shipped to Halifax, Nova Scotia on the S.S. FLORIZEL about June 8, 1912. The description reads: "bald head; dark hair; weight 160 pounds; height 5 feet 9 inches; body badly decomposed; about 50 years of age."

ACKNOWLEDGEMENTS

Since I started gathering material for this crew list, it has seen high as well as low tides. Sometimes I worked like a beaver and other times it was put aside, almost forgotten.

So many people were involved in helping me that it would be almost an impossible task to name them all.

A very, very special thanks to the Public Archives of Nova Scotia, Halifax, for tolerating my intrusion upon their time for eight days in a row. They were most helpful and kind in permitting my wife to photograph anything and everything they had pertaining to the Titanic.

To the Halifax Regional Library for making dry copies of Halifax newspapers of the period, my warmest thanks.

To the caretakers who pointed out the graves of the *Titanic* dead, a hearty handshake across the border.

My thanks to Mr. Thomas E. Appleton, Historian - Marine Administration, Ministry of Transport, Ottawa, Canada for furnishing the picture of the *Montmagny*.

Nancy Mace will always have my warmest wishes for success because she is the one who had the courage to cut the *Lloyd's List* apart and arrange it alphabetically, then type it and help me compare it with the *Senate Investigation List*, a colossal task.

My best to Jack Eaton, Historian of the Titanic Historical Society for allowing me to use his list.

My grateful thanks to Ed Kamuda, editor of TITANIC COMMUTATOR for a copy of the *Senate Investigation List*.

My eternal love to my wife, Elizabeth, for her

96

patience and understanding and for taking photos
for this list.

—Arnold Watson

TITANIC HISTORICAL SOCIETY

The **TITANIC HISTORICAL SOCIETY**, formerly known as the **TITANIC ENTHUSIASTS OF AMERICA**, was founded in 1963 for the purpose of investigating and perpetuating the history and memory of the White Star liners *Olympic, Titanic* and *Britannic* (1914). The Society is also interested in the history of the White Star Line, the people involved with that organization, and in the vessels owned by that line. Harland and Wolff, the company responsible for the building of the White Star fleet, is also of interest to the T.H.S.

Recently, the Society broadened its scope of interest to include 19th and 20th Century North Atlantic liners in general, with special emphasis on the White Star and Cunard Lines and the three vessels named above.

Membership information is available upon request from:

TITANIC HISTORICAL SOCIETY, INC.
Post Office Box 53
Indian Orchard, Massachusetts
01151-0053, U.S.A.

The *Titanic Commutator*, the official journal of the T.H.S., is published quarterly, and is paid for through membership dues to the organization. The Titanic Historical Society is recognized as a non-profit, tax-exempt educational organization under the Internal Revenue Service Code and the laws of the Commonwealth of Massachusetts. The Society maintains its archives and a public display of *Titanic* artifacts at the Philadelphia Maritime Museum, Philadelphia, Pennsylvania.

DEDICATED TO . . .
"They that go down to the sea in ships,
That do business in great waters . . ."
Psalm 107:23

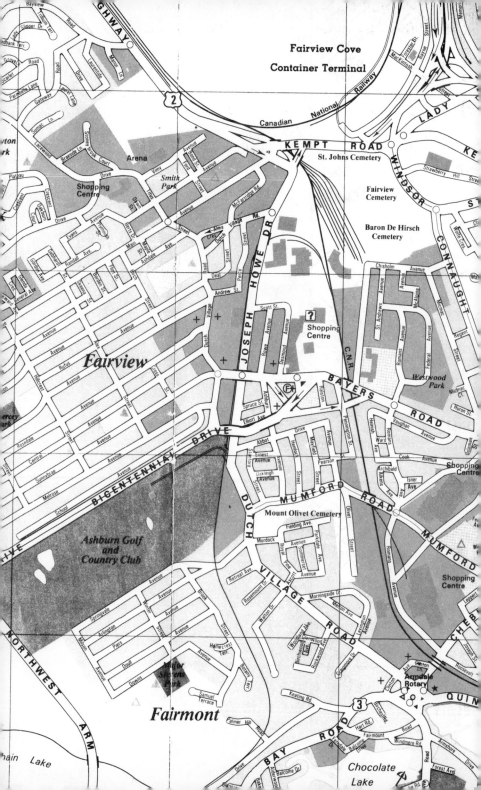